Coherent PDF
Command Line Tools

User Manual
Version 2.8 (December 2024)

Coherent Graphics Ltd

For bug reports, feature requests and comments, email
contact@coherentgraphics.co.uk

Quickstart Examples

These examples demonstrate just a few of the facilities provided by the Coherent PDF Command Line Tools. See each chapter for more commands and full details.

Chapter 1: Basic Usage

```
cpdf in.pdf 1-3,6 -o out.pdf
```

Read in.pdf, select pages 1, 2, 3 and 6, and write those pages to out.pdf.

```
cpdf in.pdf even -o out.pdf
```

Select the even pages (2, 4, 6...) from in.pdf and write those pages to out.pdf.

```
cpdf -merge in.pdf in2.pdf AND -add-text "Copyright 2024"
    -o out.pdf
```

Using AND to perform several operations in order, here merging two files together and adding a copyright stamp to every page.

```
cpdf -args args.txt
```

Read args.txt and use its contents as the command line arguments for Cpdf.

Chapter 2: Merging and Splitting

```
cpdf -merge in.pdf in2.pdf -o out.pdf
```

Merge in.pdf and in2.pdf into one document, writing to out.pdf.

```
cpdf -split in.pdf -o Chunk%%%.pdf -chunk 10
```

Split in.pdf into ten-page chunks, writing them to Chunk001.pdf, Chunk002.pdf etc.

```
cpdf -split-bookmarks 0 in.pdf -utf8 -o @B.pdf
```

Split in.pdf on bookmark boundaries, writing each to a file whose name is the bookmark label.

```
cpdf -split-max 1Mb in.pdf -o %%%.pdf
```

Split in.pdf into files of 1Mb or less

```
cpdf -spray in.pdf -o a.pdf -o b.pdf -o c.pdf
```

Split in.pdf, writing pages 1,4,7... to a.pdf, 2,5,8... to b.pdf and 3,6,9... to c.pdf.

Chapter 3: Pages

```
cpdf -scale-page "2 2" in.pdf -o out.pdf
```

Scale both the dimensions and contents of in.pdf by a factor of two in x and y directions.

```
cpdf -scale-to-fit usletterportrait in.pdf -o out.pdf
```

Scale the pages in in.pdf to fit the US Letter page size, writing to out.pdf

```
cpdf -shift "26pt 18mm" in.pdf -o out.pdf
```

Shift the contents of the page by 26 pts in the x direction, and 18 millimetres in the y direction, writing to out.pdf

```
cpdf -rotate-contents 90 in.pdf -o out.pdf
```

Rotate the contents of the pages in in.pdf by ninety degrees and write to out.pdf.

```
cpdf -cropbox "0 0 600pt 400pt" in.pdf -o out.pdf
```

Crop the pages in in.pdf to a 600 pts by 400 pts rectangle.

Chapter 4: Encryption and Decryption

```
cpdf -encrypt 128bit fred joe in.pdf -o out.pdf
```

Encrypt in.pdf using 128bit PDF encryption using the owner password fred and the user password joe and writing the encrypted file to out.pdf

```
cpdf -decrypt in.pdf owner=fred -o out.pdf
```

Decrypt in.pdf using the owner password, writing to out.pdf.

Chapter 5: Compression

```
cpdf -compress in.pdf -o out.pdf
```

Compress the data streams in in.pdf, writing the result to out.pdf.

```
cpdf -decompress in.pdf -o out.pdf
```

Decompress the data streams in in.pdf, writing to out.pdf.

```
cpdf -squeeze in.pdf -o out.pdf
```

Squeeze in.pdf, writing to out.pdf. Squeezing rearranges the structure of the PDF file to save space.

Chapter 6: Bookmarks

```
cpdf -list-bookmarks -utf8 in.pdf
```

List the bookmarks in in.pdf.

```
cpdf -add-bookmarks bookmarks.txt in.pdf -o out.pdf
```

Add bookmarks in the same form from a prepared file bookmarks.txt to in.pdf, writing to out.pdf. JSON alternatives are also available.

```
cpdf -table-of-contents in.pdf -o out.pdf
```

Typeset a table of contents from existing bookmarks and prepend to the document.

Chapter 7: Presentations

```
cpdf -presentation in.pdf 2-end -trans Split -duration 10
     -o out.pdf
```

Use the Split style to build a presentation from the PDF in.pdf, each slide staying 10 seconds on screen unless manually advanced. The first page, being a title does not move on automatically, and has no transition effect.

Chapter 8: Logos, Watermarks and Stamps

```
cpdf -stamp-on watermark.pdf in.pdf -o out.pdf
```

Stamp the file watermark.pdf on to each page of in.pdf, writing the result to out.pdf.

```
cpdf -topleft 10 -font Courier
     -add-text "Page \%Page\nDate \%d-\%m-\%Y" in.pdf -o out.pdf
```

Add a page number and date to all the pages in in.pdf using the Courier font, writing to out.pdf.

Chapter 9: Multipage Facilities

```
cpdf -impose-xy "2 1" in.pdf -o out.pdf
```

Two up impose the file in.pdf, writing to out.pdf.

```
cpdf -pad-after in.pdf 1,3,4 -o out.pdf
```

Add extra blank pages after pages one, three and four of a document.

```
cpdf -chop "2 2" in.pdf -o out.pdf
```

Chop each page into four quarters, including each in the output.

Chapter 10: Annotations

```
cpdf -list-annotations-json in.pdf > out.json
```

List the annotations in a file in.pdf to standard output, redirecting to file out.json.

```
cpdf -set-annotations-json out.json in.pdf -o out.pdf
```

Add the annotations from a JSON annotations file to in.pdf, writing to out.pdf.

```
cpdf -remove-annotations in.pdf -o out.pdf
```

Remove the annotations from in.pdf, writing to out.pdf.

Chapter 11: Document Information and Metadata

```
cpdf -info -utf8 in.pdf
```

List document metadata for in.pdf.

```
cpdf -set-title "The New Title" -also-set-xmp in.pdf -o out.pdf
```

Set the document title of in.pdf, writing to out.pdf.

```
cpdf -hide-toolbar true in.pdf -o out.pdf
```

Set the document in.pdf to open with the PDF Viewer's toolbar hidden, writing to out.pdf.

```
cpdf -set-metadata metadata.xml in.pdf -o out.pdf
```

Set the metadata in a PDF in.pdf to the contents of the file metadata.xml, and write the output to out.pdf.

```
cpdf -set-page-layout TwoColumnRight in.pdf -o out.pdf
```

Set the document in.pdf to open in PDF Viewer showing two columns of pages, starting on the right, putting the result in out.pdf.

```
cpdf -set-page-mode FullScreen in.pdf -o out.pdf
```

Set the document in.pdf to open in PDF Viewer in full screen mode, putting the result in out.pdf.

```
cpdf -print-page-labels-json in.pdf
```

Show, in JSON format, the page labels in in.pdf.

```
cpdf -composition in.pdf
```

Show how much data in in.pdf is used for images, fonts etc.

Chapter 12: File Attachments

```
cpdf -attach-file sheet.xls in.pdf -o out.pdf
```

Attach the file sheet.xls to in.pdf, writing to out.pdf.

```
cpdf -remove-files in.pdf -o out.pdf
```

Remove any attachments from in.pdf, writing to out.pdf.

```
cpdf -dump-attachments in.pdf -o /home/fred/attachments
```

Dump attachments to file, given the directory to put them in.

Chapter 13: Images

```
cpdf -image-resolution 600 in.pdf
```

Identify and list any image used at less than 600dpi.

```
cpdf -extract-images in.pdf -im /usr/bin/magick -o output/%%%
```

Extract images from in.pdf to directory output (with the help of imagemagick).

```
cpdf -process-images -jpeg-to-jpeg 65 in.pdf -o out.pdf
```

Process JPEG images in in.pdf to 65% quality, writing the output to out.pdf.

```
cpdf -gs gs -rasterize in.pdf -o out.pdf
```

Rasterize PDF page content, creating new PDF.

```
cpdf -gs gs -output-image in.pdf 10-end -o image%%%.png
```

Rasterize PDF pages to PNG files.

Chapter 14: Fonts

```
cpdf -list-fonts in.pdf
```

List the fonts in use, and what pages they are used on.

```
cpdf -missing-fonts in.pdf
```

List missing fonts.

Chapter 15: PDF and JSON

```
cpdf in.pdf -output-json -utf8 -output-json-parse-content-streams
    -o out.json
```

Write the PDF in JSON format to the given file, parsing its content streams into individual JSON objects too.

```
cpdf -j in.json -o out.pdf
```

Load a PDF in JSON format, writing to an output PDF.

Chapter 16: Optional Content Groups

```
cpdf -ocg-list in.pdf
```

List the optional content groups by name.

```
cpdf -ocg-coalesce-on-name in.pdf -o out.pdf
```

Coalesce optional content groups after merging or stamping two files with OCGs with like names.

Chapter 17: Creating New PDFs

```
cpdf -create-pdf -create-pdf-pages 20
     -create-pdf-papersize usletterportrait -o out.pdf
```

Create a US Letter PDF of twenty pages.

```
cpdf -typeset file.txt -create-pdf-papersize a3portrait
     -font Courier -font-size 10 -o out.pdf
```

Typeset a text file as PDF on A3 paper with Courier 10 point font.

```
cpdf -jpeg pic.jpeg -png pic.png -o out.pdf
```

Make a two-page PDF, the first from a JPEG and the second from a PNG.

Chapter 18: Drawing on PDFs

```
cpdf -create-pdf AND -draw -to "100 100" -line "400 400"
    -line "400 100" -close -fill
    -o out.pdf
```

Create a new PDF and draw a filled triangle on it.

```
cpdf -create-pdf AND -draw -mtrans "100 200" -font-size 50
    -leading 55 -bt -text "This is" -nl -text "on multiple"
    -nl -text "lines" -et -o out.pdf
```

Create a new PDF and draw three lines of text on it.

```
cpdf -create-pdf AND -draw -bt -text "Page 1" -et -newpage
    -bt -text "Page 2" -et -o out.pdf
```

Create a new PDF and draw text on one page and then the next.

Chapter 19: Accessible PDFs with PDF/UA

```
cpdf -verify 'PDF/UA-1(matterhorn)' -json in.pdf
```

Verify in.pdf for conformance to PDF/UA-1 using the Matterhorn protocol, returning results in JSON format.

Chapter 20: Miscellaneous

```
cpdf -blacktext in.pdf -o out.pdf
```

Blacken all the text in in.pdf, writing to out.pdf.

```
cpdf -thinlines 2pt in.pdf -o out.pdf
```

Make sure all lines in in.pdf are at least 2pts wide, writing to out.pdf.

```
cpdf -print-dict-entry /URI in.pdf
```

List all URLs in annotation hyperlinks in in.pdf.

Contents

Typographical Conventions

Command lines to be typed are shown in `typewriter font` in a box. For example:

```
cpdf in.pdf -o out.pdf
```

When describing the general form of a command, rather than a particular example, square brackets [] are used to enclose optional parts, and angled braces <> to enclose general descriptions which may be substituted for particular instances. For example,

```
cpdf <operation> in.pdf [<range>] -o out.pdf
```

describes a command line which requires an operation and, optionally, a range. An exception is that we use `in.pdf` and `out.pdf` instead of `<input file>` and `<output file>` to reduce verbosity.

Under Microsoft Windows, type `cpdf.exe` instead of `cpdf`.

Chapter 1

Basic Usage

```
-help                    --help                  -version
-o                       -i                      -idir <directory>
-recrypt                 -decrypt-force          -stdout
-stdin                   -stdin-user <password>  -stdin-owner <password>
-producer <text>         -creator <text>         -change-id
-l                       -cpdflin <filename>     -keep-l
-no-preserve-objstm      -create-objstm          -args <filename>
-args-json <filename>    -utf8                   -stripped
-raw                     -gs                     -gs-malformed
-gs-malformed-force      -gs-quiet               -error-on-malformed
```

The Coherent PDF tools provide a wide range of facilities for modifying PDF files created by other means. There is a single command-line program Cpdf (cpdf.exe under Microsoft Windows). The rest of this manual describes the options that may be given to this program.

1.1 Documentation

The operation -help / --help prints each operation and option together with a short description. The operation -version prints the Cpdf version string.

1.2 Input and Output Files

The typical pattern for usage is

```
cpdf [<operation>] <input file(s)> -o <output file>
```

and the simplest concrete example, assuming the existence of a file in.pdf is:

```
cpdf in.pdf -o out.pdf
```

This copies in.pdf to out.pdf. Of course, we should like to do more interesting things to the PDF file than that!

Files on the command line are distinguished from other input by their containing a period. If an input file does not contain a period, it should be preceded by -i. For example:

```
cpdf -i in -o out.pdf
```

A whole directory of files may be added (where a command supports multiple files) by using the -idir option:

```
cpdf -merge -idir myfiles -o out.pdf
```

The files in the directory myfiles are considered in alphabetical order. They must all be PDF files. If the names of the files are numeric, leading zeroes will be required for the order to be correct (e.g 001.pdf, 002.pdf etc).

To restrict cpdf to files ending in .pdf (in upper or lower or mixed case) add the option -idir-only-pdfs *before* -idir:

```
cpdf -merge -idir-only-pdfs -idir myfiles -o out.pdf
```

1.3   Input Ranges

An *input range* may be specified after each input file. This is treated differently by each operation. For instance

```
cpdf in.pdf 2-5 -o out.pdf
```

extracts pages two, three, four and five from in.pdf, writing the result to out.pdf, assuming that in.pdf contains at least five pages. Here are the rules for building input ranges:

- A number represents a page number

- A page label may be used in place of a number e.g [iii] represents the first page found which is labelled iii.

- A tilde (˜) defines a page number counting from the end of the document rather than the beginning. Page ˜1 is the last page, ˜2 the penultimate page etc.

- A dash (-) defines ranges, e.g. 1-5 or 6-3.

- A comma (,) allows one to specify several ranges, e.g. `1-2,4-5`.

- The word `end` represents the last page.

- The words `odd` and `even` can be used in place of or at the end of a page range to restrict to just the odd or even pages.

- The words `portrait` and `landscape` can be used in place of or at the end of a page range to restrict to just those pages which are portrait or landscape. Note that the meaning of "portrait" and "landscape" does not take account of any viewing rotation in place (use `-upright` from chapter 3 first, if required). A page with equal width and height is considered neither portrait nor landscape.

- The word `reverse` is the same as `end-1`.

- The word `all` is the same as `1-end`.

- A range must contain no spaces.

- Prepending `NOT` to a whole page range inverts it.

- Prepending `<n>DUP` to a whole page range duplicates each page of the range `<n>` times.

For example:

```
cpdf in.pdf 1,2,7-end -o out.pdf
```

Remove pages three, four, five and six from a document.

```
cpdf in.pdf 1-16odd -o out.pdf
```

Extract the odd pages 1,3,...,13,15.

```
cpdf in.pdf landscape -rotate 90 -o out.pdf
```

Rotate all landscape pages by ninety degrees.

```
cpdf in.pdf 1,all -o out.pdf
```

Duplicate the front page of a document, perhaps as a fax cover sheet.

```
cpdf in.pdf ~3-~1 -o out.pdf
```

Extract the last three pages of a document, in order.

```
cpdf in.pdf 2DUP1-10 -o out.pdf
```

Produce the pages 1,1,2,2,....10,10.

1.4   Working with Encrypted Documents

In order to perform many operations, encrypted input PDF files must be decrypted. Some require the owner password, some either the user or owner passwords. Either password is supplied by writing user=<password> or owner=<password> following each input file requiring it (before or after any range). The document will *not* be re-encrypted upon writing. For example:

```
cpdf in.pdf user=charles -info
cpdf in.pdf owner=fred reverse -o out.pdf
```

To re-encrypt the file with its existing encryption upon writing, which is required if only the user password was supplied, but allowed in any case, add the -recrypt option:

```
cpdf in.pdf user=charles reverse -recrypt -o out.pdf
```

The password required (owner or user) depends upon the operation being performed. Separate facilities are provided to decrypt and encrypt files (See Section 4).

When appropriate passwords are not available, the option -decrypt-force may be added to the command line to process the file regardless.

For decryption with AES256, passwords may be Unicode. However the password, should it contain non-ASCII characters, must be normalized by applying the SASLPrep profile (RFC 4013) of the stringprep algorithm (RFC 3454) using the Normalize and BiDi options. It must then be converted to UTF8 and truncated to 127 bytes. Cpdf does not perform this pre-processing – it takes its passwords from the command line without processing.

1.5   Standard Input and Standard Output

Thus far, we have assumed that the input PDF will be read from a file on disk, and the output written similarly. Often it's useful to be able to read input from stdin (Standard Input) or write output to stdout (Standard Output) instead. The typical use is to join several programs together into a *pipe*, passing data from one to the next without the use of intermediate files. Use -stdin to read from standard input, and -stdout to write to standard input, either to pipe data between multiple programs, or multiple invocations of the same program. For example, this sequence of commands (all typed on one line)

```
cpdf in.pdf reverse -stdout |
cpdf -stdin 1-5 -stdout |
cpdf -stdin reverse -o out.pdf
```

extracts the last five pages of in.pdf in the correct order, writing them to out.pdf. It does this by reversing the input, taking the first five pages and then reversing the result.

To supply passwords for a file from -stdin, use -stdin-owner <password> and/or -stdin-user <password>.

Using -stdout on the final command in the pipeline to output the PDF to screen is not recommended, since PDF files often contain compressed sections which are not screen-readable.

Several Cpdf operations write to standard output by default (for example, listing fonts). A useful feature of the command line (not specific to Cpdf) is the ability to redirect this output to a file. This is achieved with the > operator:

```
cpdf -info in.pdf > file.txt
```

Use the -info operation (See Section 11.1), redirecting the output to file.txt.

1.6   Doing Several Things at Once with AND

The keyword AND can be used to string together several commands in one. The advantage compared with using pipes is that the file need not be repeatedly parsed and written out, saving time.

To use AND, simply leave off the output specifier (e.g -o) of one command, and the input specifier (e.g filename) of the next. For instance:

```
cpdf -merge in.pdf in2.pdf AND -add-text "Label"
     AND -merge in3.pdf -o out.pdf
```

Merge in.pdf and in2.pdf together, add text to both pages, append in3.pdf and write to out.pdf.

To specify the range for each section, use -range:

```
cpdf -merge in.pdf in2.pdf AND -range 2-4 -add-text "Label"
     AND -merge in3.pdf -o out.pdf
```

1.7   Units

When measurements are given to Cpdf, they are in points (1 point = 1/72 inch). They may optionally be followed by some letters to change the measurement. The following are supported:

pt	Points (72 points per inch). The default.
cm	Centimeters
mm	Millimeters
in	Inches

For example, one may write 14mm or 21.6in. In addition, the following letters stand for various page dimensions:

PW	Page width
PH	Page height
PMINX	Page minimum x coordinate
PMINY	Page minimum y coordinate
PMAXX	Page maximum x coordinate
PMAXY	Page maximum y coordinate
CW	Crop box width
CH	Crop box height
CMINX	Crop box minimum x coordinate
CMINY	Crop box minimum y coordinate
CMAXX	Crop box maximum x coordinate
CMAXY	Crop box maximum y coordinate
AW	Art box width
AH	Art box height
AMINX	Art box minimum x coordinate
AMINY	Art box minimum y coordinate
AMAXX	Art box maximum x coordinate
AMAXY	Art box maximum y coordinate
TW	Trim box width
TH	Trim box height
TMINX	Trim box minimum x coordinate
TMINY	Trim box minimum y coordinate
TMAXX	Trim box maximum x coordinate
TMAXY	Trim box maximum y coordinate
BW	Bleed box width
BH	Bleed box height
BMINX	Bleed box minimum x coordinate
BMINY	Bleed box minimum y coordinate
BMAXX	Bleed box maximum x coordinate
BMAXY	Bleed box maximum y coordinate

For example, we may write PMINX PMINY to stand for the coordinate of the lower left corner of the page.

Simple arithmetic may be performed using the words add, sub, mul and div to stand for addition, subtraction, multiplication and division. For example, one may write 14in sub 30pt or PMINX mul 2

1.8   Setting the Producer and Creator

The -producer and -creator options may be added to any Cpdf command line to set the producer and/or creator of the PDF file. If the file was converted from another format, the *creator* is the program producing the original, the *producer* the program converting it to PDF.

```
cpdf -merge in.pdf in2.pdf -producer MyMerger -o out.pdf
```

Merge in.pdf and in2.pdf, setting the producer to MyMerger and writing the output to out.pdf.

1.9   PDF Version Numbers

When an operation which uses a part of the PDF standard which was introduced in a later version than that of the input file, the PDF version in the output file is set to the later version (most PDF viewers will try to load any PDF file, even if it is marked with a later version number). However, this automatic version changing may be suppressed with the -keep-version option. If you wish to manually alter the PDF version of a file, use the -set-version operation described in Section 20.5.

1.10   File IDs

PDF files contain an ID (consisting of two parts), used by some workflow systems to uniquely identify a file. To change the ID, behavior, use the -change-id operation. This will create a new ID for the output file.

```
cpdf -change-id in.pdf -o out.pdf
```

Write in.pdf to out.pdf, changing the ID.

1.11   Linearization

Linearized PDF is a version of the PDF format in which the data is held in a special manner to allow content to be fetched only when needed. This means viewing a multipage PDF over a slow connection is more responsive. By default, Cpdf does not linearize output files. To make it do so, add the -l option to the command line, in addition to any other command being used. For example:

```
cpdf -l in.pdf -o out.pdf
```

Linearize the file in.pdf, writing to out.pdf.

This requires the existence of the external program cpdflin which is provided with commercial versions of Cpdf. This must be installed as described in the installation documentation provided with your copy of cpdf. If you are unable to install cpdflin, you must use -cpdflin to let Cpdf know where to find it:

```
cpdf.exe -cpdflin "C:\\cpdflin.exe" -l in.pdf -o out.pdf
```

Linearize the file in.pdf, writing to out.pdf.

In extremis, you may place cpdflin and its resources in the current working directory, though this is not recommended. For further help, refer to the installation instructions for your copy of Cpdf.

To keep the existing linearization status of a file (produce linearized output if the input is linearized and the reverse), use -keep-l instead of -l.

1.12   Object Streams

PDF 1.5 introduced a new mechanism for storing objects to save space: object streams. by default, Cpdf will preserve object streams in input files, creating no more. To prevent the retention of existing object streams, use -no-preserve-objstm:

```
cpdf -no-preserve-objstm in.pdf -o out.pdf
```

Write the file in.pdf to out.pdf, removing any object streams.

To create new object streams if none exist, or augment the existing ones, use -create-objstm:

```
cpdf -create-objstm in.pdf -o out.pdf
```

Write the file in.pdf to out.pdf, preserving any existing object streams, and creating any new ones for new objects which have been added.

To create wholly new object streams, use both options together:

```
cpdf -create-objstm -no-preserve-objstm in.pdf -o out.pdf
```

Write the file in.pdf to out.pdf with wholly new object streams.

Files written with object streams will be set to PDF 1.5 or higher, unless -keep-version is used (see above).

1.13   Malformed Files

There are many malformed PDF files in existence, including many produced by otherwise-reputable applications. Cpdf attempts to correct these problems silently.

Grossly malformed files will be reconstructed. The reconstruction progress is shown on stderr (Standard Error):

```
$cpdf in.pdf -o out.pdf
couldn't lex object number
Attempting to reconstruct the malformed pdf in.pdf...
Read 5530 objects
Malformed PDF reconstruction succeeded!
```

In the unlikely event that Cpdf cannot reconstruct a malformed file, it is able to use the gs program to try to reconstruct the PDF file, if you have it installed. For example, if gs is installed and in your path, we might try:

```
cpdf -gs gs -gs-malformed in.pdf -o out.pdf
```

To suppress the output of gs use the -gs-quiet option. If the malformity lies inside an individual page of the PDF, rather than in its gross structure, Cpdf may appear to succeed in reconstruction, only to fail when processing a page (e.g when adding text). To force the use of gs to pre-process such files so cpdf cannot fail on them, use -gs-malformed-force:

```
cpdf in.pdf -gs gs -gs-malformed-force -o out.pdf [-gs-quiet]
```

The command line for -gs-malformed-force must be of *precisely* this form. Sometimes, on the other hand, we might wish Cpdf to fail immediately on any malformed file, rather than try its own reconstruction process. The option -error-on-malformed achieves this.

> *Note: Use of these commands with -gs is a last resort; they may strip some metadata from PDF files.*

Sometimes old, pre-ISO standardisation files can be technically well-formed but use inefficient PDF constructs. If you are sure the input files you are using are modern ISO-compliant PDFs, the -fast option may be added to the command line (or, if using AND, to each section of the command line). This will use certain shortcuts which speed up processing, but would fail on a minority of pre-ISO files. The -fast option may be used with:

```
Chapter 3
-rotate-contents -upright -vflip -hflip
-shift -scale-page -scale-to-fit -scale-contents
-show-boxes -hard-box -trim-marks

Chapter 8
-add-text -add-rectangle
-stamp-on -stamp-under -combine-pages

Chapter 9
-impose -impose-xy -twoup -twoup-stack
```

If problems occur, refrain from using -fast.

1.14   Error Handling

When Cpdf encounters an error, it exits with code 2. An error message is displayed on stderr (Standard Error). In normal usage, this means it is displayed on the screen. When a bad or inappropriate password is given, the exit code is 1.

1.15   Control Files

```
cpdf -args <filename>
cpdf -args-json <filename>
```

Some operating systems have a limit on the length of a command line. To circumvent this, or simply for reasons of flexibility, a control file may be specified from which arguments are drawn.

Using -args or will perform direct textual substitution of the file into the command line, prior to any other processing.

Using -args-json will read arguments from a JSON file consisting of a single array of strings. For example:

```
["-merge",
 "hello.pdf",
 "cpdfmanual.pdf",
 //Cpdf's JSON parser allows C-style comments
 "-o",
 /* The output file name: */
 "out.pdf"]
```

1.16   String Arguments

Command lines are handled differently on each operating system. Some characters are reserved with special meanings, even when they occur inside quoted string arguments. To avoid this problem, Cpdf performs processing on string arguments as they are read.

A backslash is used to indicate that a character which would otherwise be treated specially by the command line interpreter is to be treated literally. For example, Unix-like systems attribute a special meaning to the exclamation mark, so the command line

```
cpdf -add-text "Hello!" in.pdf -o out.pdf
```

would fail. We must escape the exclamation mark with a backslash:

```
cpdf -add-text "Hello\!" in.pdf -o out.pdf
```

It follows that backslashes intended to be taken literally must themselves be escaped (i.e. written \\).

1.17   Text Encodings

Some Cpdf commands write text to standard output, or read text from the command line or configuration files. These are:

```
-info
-list-bookmarks
-set-author et al.
-list-annotations
-dump-attachments
```

There are three options to control how the text is interpreted:

```
-utf8
-stripped
-raw
```

Add -utf8 to use Unicode UTF8, -stripped to convert to 7 bit ASCII by dropping any high characters, or -raw to perform no processing. The default unless specified in the documentation for an individual operation is -stripped.

In modern usage, -utf8 is almost always the sensible option. But for historical reasons it would be the default.

1.18   Line Endings

For historical reasons, Cpdf uses the Unix line ending character (LF) when writing text files on Microsoft Windows. For example, bookmark files.

Chapter 2

Merging and Splitting

```
cpdf -merge in1.pdf [<range>] in2.pdf [<range>] [<more names/ranges>]
     [-collate] [-collate-n <n>] [-retain-numbering]
     [-merge-add-bookmarks [-merge-add-bookmarks-use-titles]]
     [-remove-duplicate-fonts] [-process-struct-trees]
     [-subformat <subformat>]
     -o out.pdf

cpdf -split in.pdf [-chunk <chunksize>] [-process-struct-trees]
     -o <format>

cpdf -split-bookmarks <level> in.pdf [-utf8] [-process-struct-trees]
     -o <format>

cpdf -split-max <file size> in.pdf [-process-struct-trees] -o <format>

cpdf -spray in.pdf [-process-struct-trees] -o a.pdf [-o b.pdf [-o ...]]
```

2.1 Merging

The -merge operation allow the merging of several files into one. Ranges can be used to select only a subset of pages from each input file in the output. The output file consists of the concatenation of all the input pages in the order specified on the command line. Actually, the -merge can be omitted, since this is the default operation of Cpdf.

```
cpdf -merge a.pdf 1 b.pdf 2-end -o out.pdf
```

Take page one of a.pdf and all but the first page of b.pdf, merge them and produce out.pdf.

```
cpdf -merge -idir files -o out.pdf
```

Merge all files from directory files, producing out.pdf.

Merge maintains and merges bookmarks, named destinations, annotations, tagged PDF information, and so on. PDF features which cannot be merged are retained if they are from the document which first exhibits that feature.

The −collate option collates pages: that is to say, it takes the first page from the first document and its range, then the first page from the second document and its range and so on. When all first pages have been taken, it begins on the second from each range, and so on. To collate in chunks use, for example, −collate−n 2.

The −retain−numbering option keeps the PDF page numbering labels of each document intact, rather than renumbering the output pages from 1.

The −remove−duplicate−fonts option ensures that fonts used in more than one of the inputs only appear once in the output.

The −merge−add−bookmarks option adds a top-level bookmark for each file, using the filename. Any existing bookmarks are retained. The −merge−add−bookmarks−use−titles, when used in conjunction with −merge−add−bookmarks, will use the title from each PDF's metadata instead of the filename.

The −process−struct−trees option will merge structure trees (the data which forms the logical structure of the PDF). In its absence, the structure tree from the first PDF only is preserved. When merging two or more PDF/UA files, we can add −subformat PDF/UA−2 to tell Cpdf to add a top-level Document structure tree element, to conform to the PDF/UA-2 standard.

2.2   Splitting

The −split operation splits a PDF file into a number of parts which are written to file, their names being generated from a *format*. The optional −chunk option allows the number of pages written to each output file to be set.

```
cpdf -split a.pdf -o out%%%.pdf
```

Split a.pdf to the files out001.pdf, out002.pdf etc.

```
cpdf a.pdf even AND -split -chunk 10 -o dir/out%%%.pdf
```

Split the even pages of a.pdf to the files out001.pdf, out002.pdf etc. with at most ten pages in each file. The directory (folder) dir must exist.

If the output format does not provide enough numbers for the files generated, the result is unspecified. The following format operators may be used:

%, %%, %%% etc.	Sequence number padded to the number of percent signs
@F	Original filename without extension
@N	Sequence number without padding zeroes
@S	Start page of this chunk
@E	End page of this chunk
@B	Bookmark name at this page, if any.
@b<w>@	Bookmark name at this page, if any, truncated to <w> characters.

Numbers padded to a fixed width field by zeroes may be obtained for @S and @E by following them with more @ signs e.g @E@@@ for a fixed width of three.

2.3   Splitting on Bookmarks

The -split-bookmarks <level> operation splits a PDF file into a number of parts, according to the page ranges implied by the document's bookmarks. These parts are then written to file with names generated from the given format.

Level 0 denotes the top-level bookmarks, level 1 the next level (sub-bookmarks) and so on. So -split-bookmarks 1 creates breaks on level 0 and level 1 boundaries.

```
cpdf -split-bookmarks 0 a.pdf -o out%%%.pdf
```

Split a.pdf to the files out001.pdf, out002.pdf on bookmark boundaries.

There may be many bookmarks on a single page (for instance, if paragraphs are bookmarked or there are two subsections on one page). The splits calculated by -split-bookmarks ensure that each page appears in only one of the output files. It is possible to use the @ operators above, including operator @B which expands to the text of the bookmark:

```
cpdf -split-bookmarks 0 a.pdf -o @B.pdf
```

Split a.pdf on bookmark boundaries, using the bookmark text as the filename.

The bookmark text used for a name has the following characters are removed, in addition to any character with ASCII code less than 32 or equal to 126. In addition, names beginning with . are not produced.

```
           / ? < > \ : * | " ^ + =
```

The bookmark may be truncated by using the @b variant:

```
cpdf -split-bookmarks 0 a.pdf -o @b10@.pdf
```

Split a.pdf on bookmark boundaries, using the first 10 characters of bookmark text as the filename.

2.4   Splitting to Maximum Size

The -split-max operation splits a file into chunks of no more than the given size, starting at the beginning. The suffixes kB, KiB, MB, MiB, GB, and GiB may be used to give the size. For example:

```
cpdf -split-max 100kB in.pdf -o out%%%.pdf
```

Split in.pdf into parts of no more than 100kB, if possible.

Should the operation not be possible for the given size, an error message is printed and no output (not even partial output) is produced.

2.5   Spraying

Spraying is a sort of de-collation. It takes one input file, and writes pages in turn to one or more outputs:

```
cpdf -spray in.pdf -o a.pdf -o b.pdf
```

Place odd pages of the input file in one file, and the even in another.

This is the only time more than one -o is allowed.

2.6   Encrypting with Split operations

The encryption parameters described in Chapter 4 may be added to the command line to encrypt each split PDF. Similarly, the -recrypt switch described in Chapter 1 may by given to re-encrypt each file with the existing encryption of the source PDF.

2.7   Splitting and structure trees

The -process-struct-trees option used in conjunction with any splitting command will trim the structure tree (the data which forms the logical structure of the PDF) for each output file. In its absence, the structure tree is preserved wholesale in each output file.

Chapter 3

Pages

```
cpdf -scale-page "<scale x> <scale y>" [-fast] in.pdf [<range>] -o out.pdf

cpdf -scale-to-fit "<x size> <y size>" [-fast] [-prerotate]
     [-scale-to-fit-scale <scale>] in.pdf [<range>] -o out.pdf

cpdf -stretch "<x size> <y size>" [-fast] in.pdf [<range>] -o out.pdf

cpdf -center-to-fit "<x size> <y size>" in.pdf [<range>] -o out.pdf

cpdf -scale-contents [<scale>] [<position>] [-fast]
     in.pdf [<range>] -o out.pdf

cpdf -shift "<shift x> <shift y>" [-fast] in.pdf [<range>] -o out.pdf

cpdf -shift-boxes "<shift x> <shift y>" in.pdf [<range>] -o out.pdf

cpdf -rotate <angle> in.pdf [<range>] -o out.pdf

cpdf -rotateby <angle> in.pdf [<range>] -o out.pdf

cpdf -upright [-fast] in.pdf [<range>] -o out.pdf

cpdf -rotate-contents <angle> [-fast] in.pdf [<range>] -o out.pdf

cpdf -hflip [-fast] in.pdf [<range>] -o out.pdf

cpdf -vflip [-fast] in.pdf [<range>] -o out.pdf

cpdf -[media|crop|art|trim|bleed]box <boxspec> in.pdf [<range>] -o out.pdf

cpdf -remove-[crop|art|trim|bleed]box in.pdf [<range>] -o out.pdf

cpdf -frombox <boxname> -tobox <boxname> [-mediabox-if-missing]
     in.pdf [<range>] -o out.pdf

cpdf -hard-box <boxname> [-fast] in.pdf [<range>]
     [-mediabox-if-missing] -o out.pdf

cpdf -show-boxes [-fast] in.pdf [<range>] -o out.pdf

cpdf -trim-marks [-fast] in.pdf [<range>] -o out.pdf
```

3.1   Page Sizes

Any time when a page size is required, instead of writing, for instance `"210mm 197mm"` one can instead write `a4portrait`. Here is a list of supported page sizes:

```
a0portrait          a1portrait          a2portrait
a3portrait          a4portrait          a5portrait
a6portrait          a7portrait          a8portrait
a9portrait          a10portrait

a0landscape         a1landscape         a2landscape
a3landscape         a4landscape         a5landscape
a6landscape         a7landscape         a8landscape
a9landscape         a10landscape

usletterportrait    usletterlandscape
uslegalportrait     uslegallandscape
```

Note that this also works when four numbers are required: for example, when setting the mediabox `"0 0 a3landscape"` will suffice.

3.2   Scale Pages

The `-scale-page` operation scales each page in the range by the X and Y factors given. This scales both the page contents, and the page size itself. It also scales any Crop Box and other boxes (Art Box, Trim Box etc). As with several of these commands, remember to take into account any page rotation when considering what the X and Y axes relate to.

```
cpdf -scale-page "2 2" in.pdf -o out.pdf
```
Convert an A4 page to A2, for instance.

The `-scale-to-fit` operation scales each page in the range to fit a given page size, preserving aspect ratio and centring the result. If a crop box is present, it is preferred to the media box.

```
cpdf -scale-to-fit "297mm 210mm" in.pdf -o out.pdf
cpdf -scale-to-fit a4portrait in.pdf -o out.pdf
```
Scale a file's pages to fit A4 portrait.

To avoid centring, supply `-top 0`, `-bottom 0`, `-left 0` or `-right 0` as appropriate. The scale can optionally be set to a percentage of the available area, instead of filling it.

```
cpdf -scale-to-fit a4portrait -scale-to-fit-scale 0.9 in.pdf -o out.pdf
```
Scale a file's pages to fit A4 portrait, scaling the page 90% of its possible size.

The −stretch operation scales the contents to the given size without regard to aspect ratio.

```
cpdf -stretch a4landscape in.pdf -o out.pdf
```
Scale a file's pages and their content to fit A4 landscape.

The −center−to−fit operation changes the page size without scaling the contents. It centers the old page on the new page.

```
cpdf -center-to-fit a3portrait in.pdf -o out.pdf
```
Set a file's pages to the given size and center the content.

The −scale−contents operation scales the contents about the center of the crop box (or, if absent, the media box), leaving the page dimensions (boxes) unchanged.

```
cpdf -scale-contents 0.5 in.pdf -o out.pdf
```
Scale a file's contents on all pages to 50% of its original dimensions.

To scale about a point other than the center, one can use the positioning commands described in Section 8.2.4. For example:

```
cpdf -scale-contents 0.5 -topright 20 in.pdf -o out.pdf
```
Scale a file's contents on all pages to 50% of its original dimensions about a point 20pts from its top right corner.

3.3   Shift Page Contents

The −shift operation shifts the contents of each page in the range by X points horizontally and Y points vertically.

```
cpdf -shift "50 0" in.pdf even -o out.pdf
```
Shift pages to the right by 50 points (for instance, to increase the binding margin).

The −shift−boxes operation has the same effect, but operates by moving the page boxes only, avoiding processing the page contents. It is therefore faster. Of course, the numbers must be inverted, since it is the boxes being moved not the page:

```
cpdf -shift-boxes "-50 0" in.pdf even -o out.pdf
```

Shift pages to the right by 50 points (for instance, to increase the binding margin).

3.4 Rotating Pages

There are two ways of rotating pages: (1) setting a value in the PDF file which asks the viewer (e.g. Acrobat) to rotate the page on-the-fly when viewing it (use -rotate or -rotateby) and (2) actually rotating the page contents and/or the page dimensions (use -upright (described elsewhere in this chapter) afterwards or -rotate-contents to just rotate the page contents).

The possible values for -rotate and -rotate-by are 0, 90, 180 and 270, all interpreted as being clockwise. Any value may be used for -rotate-contents.

The -rotate operation sets the viewing rotation of the selected pages to the absolute value given.

```
cpdf -rotate 90 in.pdf -o out.pdf
```

Set the rotation of all the pages in the input file to ninety degrees clockwise.

The -rotateby operation changes the viewing rotation of all the given pages by the relative value given.

```
cpdf -rotateby 90 in.pdf -o out.pdf
```

Rotate all the pages in the input file by ninety degrees clockwise.

The -rotate-contents operation rotates the contents and dimensions of the page by the given relative value.

```
cpdf -rotate-contents 90 in.pdf -o out.pdf
```

Rotate all the page contents in the input file by ninety degrees clockwise. Does not change the page dimensions.

The -upright operation does whatever combination of -rotate and -rotate-contents is required to change the rotation of the document to zero without altering its appearance. In addition, it makes sure the media box has its origin at (0,0), changing other boxes to compensate. This is important because some operations in CPDF (such as scale-to-fit), and in other PDF-processing programs, work properly only when the origin is (0, 0).

```
cpdf -upright in.pdf -o out.pdf
```

Make pages upright.

3.5   Flipping Pages

The `-hflip` and `-vflip` operations flip the contents of the chosen pages horizontally or vertically. No account is taken of the current page rotation when considering what "horizontally" and "vertically" mean, so you may like to use `-upright` (see above) first.

```
cpdf -hflip in.pdf even -o out.pdf
```

Flip the even pages in `in.pdf` horizontally.

```
cpdf -vflip in.pdf -o out.pdf
```

Flip all the pages in `in.pdf` vertically.

3.6   Boxes and Cropping

All PDF files contain a *media box* for each page, giving the dimensions of the paper. To change these dimensions (without altering the page contents in any way), use the `-mediabox` operation.

```
cpdf -mediabox "0pt 0pt 500pt 500pt" in.pdf -o out.pdf
```

Set the media box to 500 points square.

The four numbers are minimum x, minimum y, width, height. x coordinates increase to the right, y coordinates increase upwards. To use absolute numbers rather than width and height we may add an initial question mark and write, for example, `?100pt 200pt 300pt 400pt` which represents the rectangle with lower-left corner (100pt, 200pt) and upper-right corner (300pt, 400pt).

PDF files can also optionally contain a *crop box* for each page, defining to what extent the page is cropped before being displayed or printed. A crop box can be set, changed and removed, without affecting the underlying media box. To set or change the crop box use `-cropbox`. To remove any existing crop box, use `-remove-cropbox`.

```
cpdf -cropbox "0pt 0pt 200mm 200mm" in.pdf -o out.pdf
```

Crop pages to the bottom left 200-millimeter square of the page.

```
cpdf -remove-cropbox in.pdf -o out.pdf
```

Remove cropping.

Note that the crop box is only obeyed in some viewers. Similar operations are available for the bleed, art, and trim boxes (`-art`, `-remove-bleed` etc.)

```
cpdf -frombox <boxname> -tobox <boxname> [-mediabox-if-missing]
    in.pdf [<range>] -o out.pdf
```

Copy the contents of one box to another.

This operation copies the contents of one box (Media box, Crop box, Trim box etc.) to another. If -mediabox-if-missing is added, the media box will be substituted when the 'from' box is not set for a given page. For example

```
cpdf -frombox /TrimBox -tobox /CropBox in.pdf -o out.pdf
```

copies the Trim Box of each page to the Crop Box of each page. The possible boxes are /MediaBox, /CropBox, /BleedBox, /TrimBox, /ArtBox.

A hard box (one which clips its contents by inserting a clipping rectangle) may be created with the -hard-box operation:

```
cpdf -hard-box /TrimBox in.pdf -o out.pdf
```

This means the resultant file may be used as a stamp without contents outside the given box reappearing. The -mediabox-if-missing option may also be used here.

3.7   Showing Boxes and Printer's Marks

The -show-boxes operation displays the boxes present on each page as method of debugging. Since boxes may be coincident, they are shown in differing colours and dash patterns so they may be identified even where they overlap. The colours are:

Media box	Red
Crop box	Green
Art box	Blue
Trim box	Orange
Bleed box	Pink

The -trim-marks operation adds trim marks to a PDF file. The trim box must be present.

Chapter 4

Encryption and Decryption

```
cpdf -encrypt <method> [-pw=]<owner> [-pw=]<user>
     [-no-encrypt-metadata] <permissions> in.pdf -o out.pdf
cpdf -decrypt [-decrypt-force] in.pdf owner=<owner password> -o out.pdf
```

4.1   Introduction

PDF files can be encrypted using various types of encryption and attaching various permissions describing what someone can do with a particular document (for instance, printing it or extracting content). There are two types of person:

The **User** can do to the document what is allowed in the permissions.

The **Owner** can do anything, including altering the permissions or removing encryption entirely.

There are five kinds of encryption:

- 40-bit encryption (method `40bit`) in Acrobat 3 (PDF 1.1) and above

- 128-bit encryption (method `128bit`) in Acrobat 5 (PDF 1.4) and above

- 128-bit AES encryption (method `AES`) in Acrobat 7 (PDF 1.6) and above

- 256-bit AES encryption (method `AES256`) in Acrobat 9 (PDF 1.7) – *this is deprecated – do not use for new documents*

- 256-bit AES encryption (method `AES256ISO`) in PDF 2.0

All encryption supports these kinds of permissions:

`-no-edit`	Cannot change the document
`-no-print`	Cannot print the document
`-no-copy`	Cannot select or copy text or graphics
`-no-annot`	Cannot add or change form fields or annotations

In addition, 128-bit encryption (Acrobat 5 and above) and AES encryption supports these:

> `-no-forms`   Cannot edit form fields
> `-no-extract`   Cannot extract text or graphics
> `-no-assemble`   Cannot merge files etc.
> `-no-hq-print`   Cannot print high-quality

Add these options to the command line to prevent each operation.

Note: Adobe Acrobat and Adobe Reader may show slightly different permissions in info dialogues – this is a result of policy changes and not a bug in Cpdf. *You may need to experiment.*

4.2   Encrypting a Document

To encrypt a document, the owner and user passwords must be given (here, `fred` and `charles` respectively):

```
cpdf -encrypt 40bit fred charles -no-print in.pdf -o out.pdf

cpdf -encrypt 128bit fred charles -no-extract in.pdf -o out.pdf

cpdf -encrypt AES fred "" -no-edit -no-copy in.pdf -o out.pdf
```

A blank user password is common. In this event, PDF viewers will typically not prompt for a password for when opening the file or for operations allowable with the user password.

```
cpdf -encrypt AES256ISO fred "" -no-forms in.pdf -o out.pdf
```

In addition, the usual method can be used to give the existing owner password, if the document is already encrypted.

The optional `-pw=` preface may be given where a password might begin with a – and thus be confused with a command line option.

When using AES encryption, the option is available to refrain from encrypting the metadata. Add `-no-encrypt-metadata` to the command line.

4.3   Decrypting a Document

To decrypt a document, the owner password is provided.

```
cpdf -decrypt in.pdf owner=fred -o out.pdf
```

The user password cannot decrypt a file.

When appropriate passwords are not available, the option `-decrypt-force` may be added to the command line to process the file regardless.

Chapter 5

Compression

```
cpdf -decompress in.pdf -o out.pdf

cpdf -compress in.pdf -o out.pdf

cpdf -squeeze in.pdf [-squeeze-log-to <filename>]
     [-squeeze-no-recompress] [-squeeze-no-pagedata] -o out.pdf
```

Cpdf provides facilities for decompressing and compressing PDF streams, and for losslessly reprocessing the whole file to 'squeeze' it. For lossy recompression of images within a PDF, see Chapter 13.

5.1   Decompressing a Document

To decompress the streams in a PDF file, for instance to manually inspect the PDF, use:

```
cpdf -decompress in.pdf -o out.pdf
```

If Cpdf finds a compression type it can't cope with, the stream is left compressed. When using -decompress, object streams are not compressed. It may be easier for manual inspection to also remove object streams, by adding the -no-preserve-objstm option to the command.

5.2   Compressing a Document

To compress the streams in a PDF file, use:

```
cpdf -compress in.pdf -o out.pdf
```

Cpdf compresses any streams which have no compression using the **FlateDecode** method, with the exception of Metadata streams, which are left uncompressed.

5.3   Squeezing a Document

To *squeeze* a PDF file, reducing its size by an average of about twenty percent (though sometimes not at all), use:

```
cpdf -squeeze in.pdf -o out.pdf
```

Adding -squeeze to the command line when using another operation will *squeeze* the file or files upon output.

   The -squeeze operation writes some information about the squeezing process to standard output. The squeezing process involves several processes which losslessly attempt to reduce the file size. It is slow, so should not be used without thought.

```
$ ./cpdf -squeeze in.pdf -o out.pdf
Initial file size is 238169 bytes
Beginning squeeze: 123847 objects
Squeezing... Down to 114860 objects
Squeezing... Down to 114842 objects
Squeezing page data
Recompressing document
Final file size is 187200 bytes,  78.60% of original.
```

The -squeeze-log-to <filename> option writes the log to the given file instead of to standard output. Log content is appended to the end of the log file, preserving existing contents.

   The option -squeeze-no-pagedata avoids the reprocessing of page data, which avoids problems in case of malformed files, and makes the process much faster at the cost of a little less compression. The option -squeeze-no-recompress is deprecated as of version 2.6 and has no effect.

Chapter 6

Bookmarks

```
cpdf -list-bookmarks [-utf8] in.pdf

cpdf -list-bookmarks-json in.pdf

cpdf -remove-bookmarks in.pdf -o out.pdf

cpdf -add-bookmarks <bookmark file> in.pdf -o out.pdf

cpdf -add-bookmarks-json <bookmark file> in.pdf -o out.pdf

cpdf -bookmarks-open-to-level <n> in.pdf -o out.pdf

cpdf -table-of-contents [-toc-title] [-toc-no-bookmark] [-toc-dot-leaders]
     [-font <font>] [-font-size <size>] in.pdf -o out.pdf
```

PDF bookmarks (properly called the *document outline*) represent a tree of references to parts of the file, typically displayed at the side of the screen. The user can click on one to move to the specified place. Cpdf provides facilities to list, add, and remove bookmarks. The format used by the list and add operations is the same, so you can feed the output of one into the other, for instance to copy bookmarks.

6.1 List Bookmarks

The -list-bookmarks operation prints (to standard output) the bookmarks in a file. The first column gives the level of the tree at which a particular bookmark is. Then the text of the bookmark in quotes. Then the page number which the bookmark points to. Then (optionally) the word "open" if the bookmark should have its children (at the level immediately below) visible when the file is loaded. Then the destination (see below). For example, upon executing

```
cpdf -list-bookmarks doc.pdf
```

the result might be:

```
0 "Part 1" 1 open
1 "Part 1A" 2 "[2 /XYZ 200 400 null]"
1 "Part 1B" 3
0 "Part 2" 4
1 "Part 2a" 5
```

If the page number is 0, it indicates that clicking on that entry doesn't move to a page.

By default, Cpdf converts unicode to ASCII text, dropping characters outside the ASCII range. To prevent this, and return unicode UTF8 output, add the -utf8 option to the command. To prevent any processing, use the -raw option. See Section 1.17 for more information. A newline in a bookmark is represented as "\n".

By using -list-bookmarks-json instead, the bookmarks are formatted as a JSON array, in order, of dictionaries formatted thus:

```
{ "level": 0,
  "text": "1 Basic Usage",
  "page": 17,
  "open": false,
  "target":
    [ { "I": 17 },
      { "N": "/XYZ" },
      { "F": 85.039 },
      { "F": 609.307 },
      null ]
  "colour": [ 0.0, 0.0, 0.0 ],
  "italic": false,
  "bold": false
}
```

Note that the colour (RGB each from 0.0 to 1.0) and shape of the text (bold, italic, or both) can be read and set with the JSON format.

See Chapter 15 for more details of Cpdf's JSON formatting. There are two differences here: bookmark text is always UTF8, and the numbers for level and page are plain, rather than begin surrounded with { "I": }.

6.1.1 Destinations

The destination is an extended description of where the bookmark should point to (i.e it can be more detailed than just giving the page). For example, it may point to a section heading halfway down a page. Here are the possibilities:

Format	Description
[*p* /XYZ *left top zoom*]	Display page number *p* with (*left*, *top*) positioned at upper-left of window and magnification of *zoom*. Writing "null" for any of *left*, *top* or *zoom* specifies no change. A *zoom* of 0 is the same as "null".
[*p* /Fit]	Display page number *p* so as to fit fully within the window.
[*p* /FitH *top*]	Display page number *p* with vertical coordinate *top* at the top of the window and the page magnified so its width fits the window. A null value for *top* implies no change.
[*p* /FitV *left*]	Display page number *p* with horizontal coordinate *left* at the left of the window, and the page magnified so its height fits the window. A null value for *left* implies no change.
[*p* /FitR *left bottom right top*]	Display page number *p* magnified so as to fit entirely within the rectangle specified by the other parameters.
[*p* /FitB]	As for /Fit but with the page's bounding box (see below).
[*p* /FitBH *top*]	As for /FitH but with the page's bounding box (see below).
[*p* /FitBV *left*]	As for /FitV but with the page's bounding box (see below).

The *bounding box* is the intersection of the page's crop box and the bounding box of the page contents. Some other kinds of destination may be produced by -list-bookmarks. They will be preserved by -add-bookmarks and may be edited as your risk.

6.2   Remove Bookmarks

The -remove-bookmarks operations removes all bookmarks from the file.

```
cpdf -remove-bookmarks in.pdf -o out.pdf
```

6.3   Add Bookmarks

The -add-bookmarks file adds bookmarks as specified by a *bookmarks file*, a text file in ASCII or UTF8 encoding and in the same format as that produced by the -list-bookmarks operation. If there are any bookmarks in the input PDF already, they are discarded. For example, if the file bookmarks.txt contains the output from -list-bookmarks above, then the command

```
cpdf -add-bookmarks bookmarks.txt in.pdf -o out.pdf
```

adds the bookmarks to the input file, writing to `out.pdf`. An error will be given if the bookmarks file is not in the correct form (in particular, the numbers in the first column which specify the level must form a proper tree with no entry being more than one greater than the last).

Bookmarks in JSON format (see above) may be added with `-add-bookmarks-json`:

```
cpdf -add-bookmarks-json bookmarks.json in.pdf -o out.pdf
```

Remember that strings in JSON bookmark files are in UTF8.

6.4   Opening bookmarks

As an alternative to extracting a bookmark file and manipulating the open-status of bookmarks, mass manipulation may be achieved by the following operation:

```
cpdf -bookmarks-open-to-level <level> in.pdf -o out.pdf
```

A level of 0 will close all bookmarks, level 1 will open just the top level, closing all others etc. To open all of them, pick a sufficiently large level.

6.5   Making a Table of Contents

Cpdf can automatically generate a table of contents from existing bookmarks, adding it to the beginning of the document.

```
cpdf -table-of-contents in.pdf -o out.pdf
```

The page(s) added will have the same dimensions, media and crop boxes as the first page of the original file. The default title is "Table of Contents", though this may be changed:

```
cpdf -table-of-contents -toc-title "Contents" in.pdf -o out.pdf
```

An empty title removes the title. The sequence \n may be used to split the title into lines. The default font is 12pt Times Roman (and 24pt for the title). The base font and size may be changed with `-font` and `-font-size` (see Section 8.2.5 for full details):

```
cpdf -table-of-contents -font "Courier-Bold" -font-size 8
     in.pdf -o out.pdf
```

Dot leaders may be added with `-toc-dot-leaders`:

```
cpdf -table-of-contents -toc-dot-leaders in.pdf -o out.pdf
```

By default, an entry for the new table of contents will be added to the document's bookmarks. To suppress this behaviour, add -toc-no-bookmark:

```
cpdf -table-of-contents -toc-no-bookmark in.pdf -o out.pdf
```

Chapter 7

Presentations

```
cpdf -presentation in.pdf [<range>] -o out.pdf
                  [-trans <transition-name>] [-duration <float>]
                  [-vertical] [-outward] [-direction <int>]
                  [-effect-duration <float>]
```

The PDF file format, starting at Version 1.1, provides for simple slide-show presentations in the manner of Microsoft Powerpoint. These can be played in Acrobat and possibly other PDF viewers, typically started by entering full-screen mode. The -presentation operation allows such a presentation to be built from any PDF file.

The -trans option chooses the transition style. When a page range is used, it is the transition *from* each page named which is altered. The following transition styles are available:

Split Two lines sweep across the screen, revealing the new page. By default the lines are horizontal. Vertical lines are selected by using the -vertical option.

Blinds Multiple lines sweep across the screen, revealing the new page. By default the lines are horizontal. Vertical lines are selected by using the -vertical option.

Box A rectangular box sweeps inward from the edges of the page. Use -outward to make it sweep from the center to the edges.

Wipe A single line sweeps across the screen from one edge to the other in a direction specified by the -direction option.

Dissolve The old page dissolves gradually to reveal the new one.

Glitter The same as **Dissolve** but the effect sweeps across the page in the direction specified by the -direction option.

To remove a transition style currently applied to the selected pages, omit the -trans option.

The `-effect-duration` option specifies the length of time in seconds for the transition itself. The default value is one second.

The `-duration` option specifies the maximum time in seconds that the page is displayed before the presentation automatically advances. The default, in the absence of the `-duration` option, is for no automatic advancement.

The `-direction` option (for **Wipe** and **Glitter** styles only) specifies the direction of the effect. The following values are valid:

0 Left to right

90 Bottom to top (**Wipe** only)

180 Right to left (**Wipe** only)

270 Top to bottom

315 Top-left to bottom-right (**Glitter** only)

For example:

```
cpdf -presentation in.pdf 2-end -trans Split -duration 10 -o out.pdf
```

The **Split** style, with vertical lines, and each slide staying ten seconds unless manually advanced. The first page (being a title) does not move on automatically, and has no transition effect.

To use different options on different page ranges, run Cpdf multiple times on the file using a different page range each time.

Chapter 8

Watermarks and Stamps

```
cpdf -stamp-on source.pdf
    [-scale-stamp-to-fit] [<positioning command>] [-relative-to-cropbox]
    in.pdf [<range>] [-fast] -o out.pdf

cpdf -stamp-under source.pdf
    [-scale-stamp-to-fit] [<positioning command>] [-relative-to-cropbox]
    in.pdf [<range>] [-fast] -o out.pdf

cpdf -combine-pages over.pdf under.pdf
    [-fast] [-prerotate] [-no-warn-rotate] -o out.pdf

cpdf ([-add-text <text-format> | -add-rectangle <size>])
    [-font <fontname>]            [-font-size <size-in-points>]
    [-load-ttf <name>=<file>]     [-embed-std14]
    [-color <color>]              [-line-spacing <number>]
    [-outline]                    [-linewidth <number>]
    [-underneath]                 [-relative-to-cropbox]
    [-prerotate]                  [-no-warn-rotate]
    [-bates <number>]             [-bates-at-range <number>]
    [-bates-pad-to <number>]      [-opacity <number>]
    [-midline]                    [-topline]
    [-fast]
    in.pdf [<range>] -o out.pdf
```

See also positioning commands below.

```
cpdf -remove-text in.pdf [<range>] -o out.pdf

cpdf -prepend-content <content> in.pdf [<range>] -o out.pdf

cpdf -postpend-content <content> in.pdf [<range>] -o out.pdf

cpdf -stamp-as-xobject stamp.pdf in.pdf [<range>] -o out.pdf
```
NB: See discussion of -fast in Section 1.13.

8.1   Add a Watermark or Logo

The -stamp-on and -stamp-under operations stamp the first page of a source PDF onto or under each page in the given range of the input file. For example,

```
cpdf -stamp-on logo.pdf in.pdf odd -o out.pdf
```

stamps the file logo.pdf onto the odd pages of in.pdf, writing to out.pdf. A watermark should go underneath each page:

```
cpdf -stamp-under topsecret.pdf in.pdf -o out.pdf
```

The position commands in Section 8.2.4 can be used to locate the stamp more precisely (they are calculated relative to the crop box of the stamp). Or, preprocess the stamp with -shift first.

The -scale-stamp-to-fit option can be added to scale the stamp to fit the page before applying it. The use of positioning commands together with -scale-stamp-to-fit is not recommended.

The -combine-pages operation takes two PDF files and stamps each page of one over each page of the other. The length of the output is the same as the length of the "under" file. For instance:

```
cpdf -combine-pages over.pdf under.pdf -o out.pdf
```

Page attributes (such as the display rotation) are taken from the "under" file. For best results, remove any rotation differences in the two files using -upright first, or by adding -prerotate to the command.

The -relative-to-cropbox option takes the positioning command to be relative to the crop box of each page rather than the media box.

8.2   Stamp Text, Dates and Times.

The -add-text operation allows text, dates and times to be stamped over one or more pages of the input at a given position and using a given font, font size and color.

```
cpdf -add-text "Copyright 2014 ACME Corp." in.pdf -o out.pdf
```

The default is black 12pt Times New Roman text in the top left of each page. The text can be placed underneath rather than over the page by adding the -underneath option.

Text previously added by Cpdf may be removed by the -remove-text operation.

```
cpdf -remove-text in.pdf -o out.pdf
```

8.2.1 Page Numbers and other Special Codes

There are various special codes to include the page number in the text:

%Page	Page number in arabic notation (1, 2, 3…)
%PageDiv2	Page number in arabic notation divided by two
%roman	Page number in lower-case roman notation (i, ii, iii…)
%Roman	Page number in upper-case roman notation (I, II, III…)
%EndPage	Last page of document in arabic notation
%Label	The page label of the page
%EndLabel	The page label of the last page
%filename	The full file name of the input document
%URL[text|URL]	Add text, which links to URL (does not work for diagonal text)
%Bookmark<n>	Bookmark text at level n (0, 1, 2, 3, 4)

For example, the format "Page %Page of %EndPage" might become "Page 5 of 17".

NB: In some circumstances (e.g in batch files) on Microsoft Windows, % is a special character, and must be escaped (written as %%). Consult your local documentation for details.

Bookmark text refers to the first bookmark of the given level on the stamped page or, if none, the last bookmark text of that level before that page, so long as uninterrupted by a bookmark of lower level. In other words, these specials are suitable for adding running heads to a document.

8.2.2 Date and Time Formats

%a	Abbreviated weekday name (Sun, Mon etc.)
%A	Full weekday name (Sunday, Monday etc.)
%b	Abbreviated month name (Jan, Feb etc.)
%B	Full month name (January, February etc.)
%d	Day of the month (01–31)
%e	Day of the month (1–31)
%H	Hour in 24-hour clock (00–23)
%I	Hour in 12-hour clock (01–12)
%j	Day of the year (001–366)
%m	Month of the year (01–12)
%M	Minute of the hour (00–59)
%p	"a.m" or "p.m"
%S	Second of the minute (00–61)
%T	Same as %H:%M:%S
%u	Weekday (1–7, 1 = Sunday)
%w	Weekday (0–6, 0 = Sunday)
%Y	Year (0000–9999)
%%	The % character.

8.2.3   Bates Numbers

Unique page identifiers can be specified by putting `%Bates` in the format. The starting point can be set with the `-bates` option. For example:

```
cpdf -add-text "Page ID: %Bates" -bates 23745 in.pdf -o out.pdf
```

To specify that bates numbering begins at the first page of the range, use `-bates-at-range` instead. This option must be specified after the range is specified. To pad the bates number up to a given number of leading zeros, use `-bates-pad-to` in addition to either `-bates` or `-bates-at-range`.

8.2.4   Position

The position of the text may be specified in absolute terms:

```
-pos-center "200 200"
```

Position the center of the baseline text at (200pt, 200pt)

```
-pos-left "200 200"
```

Position the left of the baseline of the text at (200pt, 200pt)

```
-pos-right "200 200"
```

Position the right of the baseline of the text at (200pt, 200pt)

Position may be set relative to certain common points:

`-top 10`	Center of baseline 10 pts down from the top center
`-topleft 10`	Left of baseline 10 pts down and in from top left
`-topleft "10 20"`	Left of baseline 10 pts down and 20 pts in from top left
`-topright 10`	Right of baseline 10 pts down and left from top right
`-topright "10 20"`	Right of baseline 10 pts down and 20 pts left from top right
`-left 10`	Left of baseline 10 pts in from center left
`-bottomleft 10`	Left of baseline 10 pts in and up from bottom left
`-bottomleft "10 20"`	Left of baseline 10 pts in and 20 pts up from bottom left
`-bottom 10`	Center of baseline 10 pts up from bottom center
`-bottomright 10`	Right of baseline 10 pts up and in from bottom right
`-bottomright "10 20"`	Right of baseline 10 pts up and 20 pts in from bottom right
`-right 10`	Right of baseline 10 pts in from the center right
`-diagonal`	Diagonal, bottom left to top right, centered on page
`-reverse-diagonal`	Diagonal, top left to bottom right, centered on page
`-center`	Centered on page

No attempt is made to take account of the page rotation when interpreting the position, so -prerotate may be added to the command line if the file contains pages with a non-zero viewing rotation (to silence the rotation warning, add -no-warn-rotate instead) This is equivalent to pre-processing the document with -upright (see chapter 3).

The -relative-to-cropbox modifier can be added to the command line to make these measurements relative to the crop box instead of the media box. The -midline option may be added to specify that the positioning commands above are to be considered relative to the midline of the text, rather than its baseline. Similarly, the -topline option may be used to specify that the position is taken relative to the top of the text.

8.2.5 Font and Size

The standard PDF fonts may be set with the -font option. They are:

Times-Roman
Times-Bold
Times-Italic
Times-BoldItalic
Helvetica
Helvetica-Bold
Helvetica-Oblique
Helvetica-BoldOblique
Courier
Courier-Bold
Courier-Oblique
Courier-BoldOblique

For example, page numbers in Times Italic can be achieved by:

```
cpdf -add-text "-%Page-" -font "Times-Italic" in.pdf -o out.pdf
```

The font size can be altered with the -font-size option, which specifies the size in points:

```
cpdf -add-text "-%Page-" -font-size 36 in.pdf -o out.pdf
```

Adding -embed-std14 <directory>, given a directory holding the URW Base35 free fonts, will embed subsetted font files in the PDF for any of the Standard fonts used. These free fonts may be downloaded from https://github.com/ArtifexSoftware/urw-base35-fonts. This is important, for example, for PDF/A documents, which must have their fonts embedded.

The standard fonts cover only the Latin characters, and are limiting. Other TrueType fonts may be introduced with the -load-ttf option, giving a name for, and the file name of the font. For example:

```
cpdf -load-ttf A=NotoSans-Black.ttf -font A -add-text "-%Page-" -o out.pdf
```

Here we have used the Noto Sans font from Google. This and other Google fonts contain characters for a huge number of scripts, and are available free from https://fonts.google.com/noto/. But you may use any TrueType font.

See Section 14.3 for how to use an existing font from the source document.

8.2.6   Colors

The -color option takes an RGB (3 values), CMYK (4 values), or Grey (1 value) color. Components range between 0 and 1. All the standard web colours https://www.w3.org/wiki/CSS/Properties/color/keywords are provided as RGB components, and may be selected by name.

```
cpdf -add-text "Hullo" -color darkgrey in.pdf -o out.pdf

cpdf -add-text "Hullo" -color "0.5 0.5 0.5" in.pdf -o out.pdf

cpdf -add-text "Hullo" -color "0.75" in.pdf -o out.pdf

cpdf -add-text "Hullo" -color "0.5 0.5 0.4 0.9" in.pdf -o out.pdf
```

Partly-transparent text may be specified using the -opacity option. Wholly opaque is 1 and wholly transparent is 0. For example:

```
cpdf -add-text "DRAFT" -color "red" -opacity 0.3 -o out.pdf
```

8.2.7   Outline Text

The -outline option sets outline text. The line width (default 1pt) may be set with the -linewidth option. For example, to stamp documents as drafts:

```
cpdf -add-text "DRAFT" -diagonal -outline in.pdf -o out.pdf
```

8.2.8   Multi-line Text

The code \n can be included in the text string to move to the next line. In this case, the vertical position refers to the baseline of the first line of text (if the position is at the top, top left or top right of the page) or the baseline of the last line of text (if the position is at the bottom, bottom left or bottom right).

```
cpdf -add-text "Specification\n%Page of %EndPage"
     -topright 10 in.pdf -o out.pdf
```

The -midline option may be used to make these vertical positions relative to the midline of a line of text rather than the baseline, as usual.

The -line-spacing option can be used to increase or decrease the line spacing, where a spacing of 1 is the standard.

```
cpdf -add-text "Specification\n%Page of %EndPage"
      -topright 10 -line-spacing 1.5 in.pdf -o out.pdf
```

Justification of multiple lines is handled by the -justify-left, -justify-right and -justify-center options. The defaults are left justification for positions relative to the left hand side of the page, right justification for those relative to the right, and center justification for positions relative to the center of the page. For example:

```
cpdf -add-text "Long line\nShort" -justify-right in.pdf -o out.pdf
```

8.2.9 Special Characters

If your command line allows for the inclusion of unicode characters, the input text will be considered as UTF8 by Cpdf. Special characters which exist in the PDF WinAnsiEncoding Latin 1 code (such as many accented characters) will be reproduced in the PDF. This does not mean, however, that every special character can be reproduced – it must exist in the font. When using a custom font, Cpdf will attempt to convert from UTF8 to the encoding of that font automatically.

(For compatibility with previous versions of cpdf, special characters may be introduced manually with a backslash followed by the three-digit octal code of the character in the PDF WinAnsiEncoding Latin 1 Code. The full table is included in Appendix D of the Adobe PDF Reference Manual, which is available at https://wwwimages2.adobe.com/content/ dam/acom/en/devnet/pdf/pdfs/PDF32000_2008.pdf. For example, a German sharp s (ß) may be introduced by \337. *This functionality was withdrawn as of version 2.6*)

8.3 Stamping Rectangles

A rectangle may be placed on one or more pages by using the -add-rectangle <size> command. Most of the options discussed above for text placement apply in the same way. For example:

```
cpdf -add-rectangle "200 300" -pos-right 30 -color red -outline
                   in.pdf -o out.pdf
```

This can be used to blank out or highlight part of the document. The following positioning options work as you would expect: -topleft, -top, -topright, -right, -bottomright, -bottom, -bottomleft, -left, -center. When using the option -pos-left "x y", the point (x, y) refers to the bottom-left of the rectangle. When using the option -pos-right "x y", the point (x, y) refers to the bottom-right of the rectangle. When using the option -pos-center "x y", the point (x, y) refers to the center of the rectangle. The options -diagonal and -reverse-diagonal have no meaning.

8.4   Low-level facilities

These two operations add content directly to the beginning or end of the page data for a page. You must understand the PDF page description language to use these.

```
cpdf -prepend-content <content> in.pdf [<range>] -o out.pdf

cpdf -postpend-content <content> in.pdf [<range>] -o out.pdf
```

The -fast option may be added (see Chapter 1). The -stamp-as-xobject operation puts a file in another as a Form XObject on the given pages. You can then use -prepend-content or -postpend-content to use it.

```
cpdf -stamp-as-xobject stamp.pdf in.pdf [<range>] -o out.pdf
```

Chapter 9

Multipage Facilities

```
cpdf -pad-before in.pdf [<range>] [-pad-with pad.pdf] -o out.pdf

cpdf -pad-after in.pdf [<range>] [-pad-with pad.pdf] -o out.pdf

cpdf -pad-every [<integer>] in.pdf [-pad-with pad.pdf] -o out.pdf

cpdf -pad-multiple [<integer>] in.pdf -o out.pdf

cpdf -pad-multiple-before [<integer>] in.pdf -o out.pdf

cpdf -redact [-process-struct-trees] in.pdf [<range>] -o out.pdf

cpdf [-impose <pagesize> | impose-xy "<x> <y>"]
     [-impose-columns] [-impose-rtl] [-impose-btt]
     [-impose-margin <margin>] [-impose-spacing <spacing>]
     [-impose-linewidth <width>] [-fast]
     in.pdf -o out.pdf

cpdf -twoup-stack [-fast] in.pdf -o out.pdf

cpdf -twoup [-fast] in.pdf -o out.pdf

cpdf -chop "<x> <y>" [-chop-columns] [-chop-rtl] [-chop-btt]
     in.pdf [<range>] -o out.pdf

cpdf [-chop-h <y> | -chop-v <x>] [-chop-columns]
     in.pdf [<range>] -o out.pdf
```

9.1 Inserting Blank Pages

Sometimes, for instance to get a printing arrangement right, it's useful to be able to insert blank pages into a PDF file. Cpdf can add blank pages before a given page or pages, or after. The pages in question are specified by a range in the usual way:

```
cpdf -pad-before in.pdf 1 -o out.pdf
```

Add a blank page before page 1 (i.e. at the beginning of the document.)

```
cpdf -pad-after in.pdf 2,16,38,84,121,147 -o out.pdf
```

Add a blank page after pages 2, 16, 38, 84, 121 and 147 (for instance, to add a clean page between chapters of a document.)

The dimensions of the padded page are derived from the boxes (media box, crop box etc.) of the page after or before which the padding is to be applied.

The -pad-every n operation places a blank page after every n pages, excluding any last one. For example on a 9 page document this command adds a blank page after pages 3 and 6:

```
cpdf -pad-every 3 in.pdf -o out.pdf
```

Add a blank page after every three pages

In all three of these operations, one may specify -pad-with providing a (usually one-page) PDF file to be used instead of a blank page. For example, a page saying "This page left intentionally blank".

The -pad-multiple n operation adds blank pages so the document has a multiple of n pages. For example:

```
cpdf -pad-multiple 8 in.pdf -o out.pdf
```

Add blank pages to in.pdf so it has a multiple of 8 pages.

The -pad-multiple-before n operation adds the padding pages at the beginning of the file instead.

9.2 Redaction

Cpdf has basic redaction facilities to remove whole pages. We simply give the page range, and such pages will be emptied of content, and any annotations and page resources removed. The page dimensions remain the same.

```
cpdf -redact in.pdf 1,2,19-end -o out.pdf
```

Redact pages 1,2 and 19-end of in.pdf, writing to out.pdf

If -process-struct-trees is added to the command, the document's structure tree will be shorn of any parts which are marked as relating to the now-redacted pages.

9.3 Imposition

Imposition is the act of putting two or more pages of an input document onto each page of the output document. There are two operations provided by Cpdf:

- the −impose operation which, given a page size fits multiple pages into it; and

- the −impose-xy operation which, given an x and y value, builds an output page which fits x input pages horizontally and y input pages vertically.

```
cpdf -impose a0landscape in.pdf -o out.pdf
```

Impose as many pages as will fit on to new A0 landscape pages.

```
cpdf -impose-xy "3 4" in.pdf -o out.pdf
```

Impose 3 across and 4 down on to new pages of 3 times the width and 4 times the height of the input ones.

The x value for −impose-xy may be set to zero to indicate an infinitely-wide page; the y value to indicate an infinitely-long one. In both cases, the pages in the input file are assumed to be of the same dimensions.

The following options may be used to modify the output:

- −impose-columns Lay the pages out in columns rather than rows.

- −impose-rtl Lay the pages out right-to-left.

- −impose-btt Lay the pages out bottom-to-top.

- −impose-margin <margin> Add a margin around the edge of the page of the given width. When using −impose-xy the page size increases; with −impose the pages are scaled.

- −impose-spacing <spacing> Add spacing between each row and column. When using −impose-xy the page size increases; with −impose the pages are scaled.

- −impose-linewidth <width> Add a border around each input page. With −impose the pages are scaled after the border is added, so you must account for this yourself.

To impose with rotated pages, for example to put two A4 portrait pages two-up on an A3 landscape page, rotate them prior to imposition.

Two other ways of putting multiple pages on a single page remain from earlier versions of Cpdf which lacked a general imposition operation. The −twoup-stack operation puts two logical pages on each physical page, rotating them 90 degrees to do so. The new mediabox is thus larger. The −twoup operation does the same, but scales the new sides down so that the media box is unchanged.

```
cpdf -twoup in.pdf -o out.pdf
```

Impose a document two-up, keeping the existing page size.

```
cpdf -twoup-stack in.pdf -o out.pdf
```

Impose a document two-up on a larger page by rotation.

NB: For all imposition options, see also discussion of −fast in Section 1.13.

9.4   Chopping up pages

The −chop operation cuts up a page into multiple pages, according to the chosen grid, and those pages replace the originals in the PDF. It is a sort of de-imposition. For example:

```
cpdf -chop "2 3" in.pdf -o out.pdf
```

Chop each page into six.

The crop box is used if present; if not, the media box. By default, the pieces are arranged in the output file row by row, and from left to right on each row. To alter this, add one or more of −chop−columns, −chop−rtl (right to left), and −chop−btt (bottom to top).

   As an alternative, pages can be chopped into two at a given position, horizontally with −chop−h or vertically with −chop−v:

```
cpdf -chop-h 400 in.pdf -o out.pdf
```

Chop each page into two, top and bottom, at 400pt mark.

To reverse the order of pages in the output, specify −chop−columns in addition.

Chapter 10

Annotations

```
cpdf -list-annotations in.pdf [<range>]

cpdf -list-annotations-json in.pdf [<range>]

cpdf -set-annotations-json <filename> [-underneath]
    in.pdf [<range>] -o out.pdf

cpdf -copy-annotations from.pdf to.pdf [<range>] -o out.pdf

cpdf -remove-annotations in.pdf [<range>] -o out.pdf
```

10.1   Listing Annotations

The -list-annotations operation prints the textual content of any annotations on the selected pages to standard output. Each annotation is preceded by the page number and followed by a newline. The output of this operation is always UTF8.

```
cpdf -list-annotations in.pdf > annots.txt
```

Print annotations from in.pdf, redirecting output to annots.txt.

More information can be obtained by listing annotations in JSON format:

```
cpdf -list-annotations-json in.pdf > annots.json
```

Print annotations from in.pdf in JSON format, redirecting output to annots.json.

This produces an array of (page number, object number, annotation) triples giving the PDF structure of each annotation. Destination pages for page links will have page numbers in place of internal PDF page links, but the content is otherwise unaltered. Here is an example entry for an annotation with object number 102 on page 10:

```
[
10, 102
{ "/H": { "N": "/I" },
  "/Border": [ { "I": 0 }, { "I": 0 }, { "I": 0 } ],
  "/Rect": [
     { "F": 89.88023 }, { "F": 409.98401 }, { "F": 323.90561 }, {
       "F": 423.32059 } ],
  "/Subtype": { "N": "/Link" },
  "/Type": { "N": "/Annot" },
  "/A": {
     "/S": { "N": "/URI" },
     "/URI": { "U" : "http://www.google.com/" },
  "/StructParent": { "I": 10 } }
]
```

Extra objects required for annotations, but which are not annotations themselves are also extracted. They omit the page number, being just a pair of the object number and object. The CPDFJSON format is described on page 77. There is an additional object, -1, which gives the Cpdf annotation format version, currently 1.

10.2   Setting annotations

We can also set annotations from a JSON file, either modified from the output of -list-annotations-json or produced manually:

---

cpdf -set-annotations annots.json in.pdf -o out.pdf

Add the annotations in annots.json on top of any already present in in.pdf, writing to out.pdf.

If replacing rather than adding annotations, use -remove-annotations first to clear the existing ones.

10.3   Copying Annotations

The -copy-annotations operation copies the annotations in the given page range from one file (the file specified immediately after the option) to another pre-existing PDF. The range is specified after this pre-existing PDF. The result is then written an output file, specified in the usual way.

---

cpdf -copy-annotations from.pdf to.pdf 1-10 -o result.pdf

Copy annotations from the first ten pages of from.pdf onto the PDF file to.pdf, writing the result to results.pdf.

It exists for historical reasons, and is no different from listing and setting the annotations using -list-annotations-json and -set-annotations.

10.4   Removing Annotations

The `-remove-annotations` operation removes all annotations from the given page range.

```
cpdf -remove-annotations in.pdf 1 -o out.pdf
```
Remove annotations from the first page of a file only.

Chapter 11

Document Information and Metadata

```
cpdf -info[-json] [-utf8] [-in | -cm | -mm] in.pdf

cpdf -page-info[-json] [-in | -cm | -mm] in.pdf [<range>]

cpdf -pages in.pdf

cpdf -set-title <title of document>
     [-also-set-xmp] [-just-set-xmp] in.pdf -o out.pdf
```
(Also -set-author etc. See Section 11.2.)
```
cpdf -set-page-layout <layout> in.pdf -o out.pdf

cpdf -set-page-mode <mode> in.pdf -o out.pdf
cpdf -set-non-full-screen-page-mode <mode> in.pdf -o out.pdf

cpdf -hide-toolbar <true | false> in.pdf -o out.pdf
     -hide-menubar
     -hide-window-ui
     -fit-window
     -center-window
     -display-doc-title

cpdf -open-at-page <page number> in.pdf -o out.pdf
cpdf -open-at-page-fit <page number> in.pdf -o out.pdf
cpdf -open-at-page-custom <destination> in.pdf -o out.pdf

cpdf -set-language <language> in.pdf -o out.pdf

cpdf -set-metadata <metadata-file> in.pdf -o out.pdf
cpdf -remove-metadata in.pdf -o out.pdf
cpdf -print-metadata in.pdf
cpdf -create-metadata in.pdf -o out.pdf
cpdf -set-metadata-date <date> in.pdf -o out.pdf

cpdf -add-page-labels in.pdf -o out.pdf
     [-label-style <style>] [-label-prefix <string>]
```

```
      [-label-startval <integer>] [-labels-progress]

cpdf -remove-page-labels in.pdf -o out.pdf
cpdf -print-page-labels[-json] in.pdf

cpdf -composition[-json] in.pdf
```

11.1   Reading Document Information

The -info operation prints entries from the document information dictionary, and from any
XMP metadata to standard output.

```
$cpdf -info pdf_reference.pdf
Encryption: Not encrypted
Permissions:
Linearized: true
Object streams: true
ID: <0b1f990718e2a92c0c112fbf08b233fb> <b2f1dbee369e11d9b951000393c97fd8>
Version: 1.5
Pages: 1236
Title: PDF Reference, version 1.6
Author: Adobe Systems Incorporated
Subject: Adobe Portable Document Format (PDF)
Keywords:
Creator: FrameMaker 7.0
Producer: Acrobat Distiller 6.0.1 for Macintosh
Created: D:20041114084116Z
Modified: D:20041114163850-08'00'
Trapped: False
PageMode: UseOutlines
PageLayout:
OpenAction: [1/XYZ -32768 -32768 1]
HideToolbar:
HideMenubar:
HideWindowUI:
FitWindow:
CenterWindow:
DisplayDocTitle: True
NonFullScreenPageMode:
AcroForm: False
XFA: False
Marked: False
UserProperties: False
Suspects: False
MediaBox: 0.000000 0.000000 612.000000 792.000000
CropBox: 41.000000 63.000000 572.000000 729.000000
```

```
BleedBox:
TrimBox: various
ArtBox: various
Subformats:
Language: en-us
XMP dc:title: PDF Reference, version 1.6
XMP dc:creator: Adobe Systems Incorporated
XMP dc:description: Adobe Portable Document Format (PDF)
```

The details of the format for creation and modification dates can be found in Appendix A. If page boxes vary among pages, the entry will read various. Add -in, -cm or mm to print boxes in inches, centimetres, or millimetres instead of points.

By default, Cpdf strips to ASCII, discarding character codes in excess of 127. In order to preserve the original unicode, add the -utf8 option. To disable all post-processing of the string, add -raw. See Section 1.17 for more information.

The -info-json operation prints the information in JSON format instead. For example:

```
{
  "Encryption": "Not encrypted",
  "Permissions": [],
  "Linearized": true,
  "Object streams": true,
  "ID": [
    "0b1f990718e2a92c0c112fbf08b233fb", "b2f1dbee369e11d9b951000393c97fd8"
  ],
  "Version": [ 1, 5 ],
  "Pages": 1236,
  "Title": "PDF Reference, version 1.6",
  "Author": "Adobe Systems Incorporated",
  "Subject": "Adobe Portable Document Format (PDF)",
  "Keywords": null,
  "Creator": "FrameMaker 7.0",
  "Producer": "Acrobat Distiller 6.0.1 for Macintosh",
  "Created": "D:20041114084116Z",
  "Modified": "D:20041114163850-08'00'",
  "Trapped": false,
  "PageMode": "UseOutlines",
  "PageLayout": null,
  "OpenAction":
    [{ "I": 1 }, { "N": "/XYZ" }, { "I": -32768 },
     { "I": -32768 }, { "I": 1 }]
  "HideToolbar": null,
  "HideMenubar": null,
  "HideWindowUI": null,
  "FitWindow": null,
  "CenterWindow": null,
```

```
    "DisplayDocTitle": true,
    "NonFullPageScreenMode": null,
    "AcroForm": false,
    "XFA": false,
    "Marked": false,
    "UserProperties": false,
    "Suspects": false,
    "MediaBox": [ 0.0, 0.0, 612.0, 792.0 ],
    "CropBox": [ 41.0, 63.0, 572.0, 729.0 ],
    "BleedBox": null,
    "TrimBox": "various",
    "ArtBox": "various",
    "Subformats": [],
    "Language": "en-us"
    "XMP dc:title": "PDF Reference, version 1.6",
    "XMP dc:creator": "Adobe Systems Incorporated",
    "XMP dc:description": "Adobe Portable Document Format (PDF)"
}
```

The -page-info operation prints the page label, media box and other boxes, and number of annotations page-by-page to standard output, for all pages in the current range.

```
$cpdf -page-info 14psfonts.pdf
Page 1:
Label: i
MediaBox: 0.000000 0.000000 600.000000 450.000000
CropBox: 200.000000 200.000000 500.000000 500.000000
BleedBox:
TrimBox:
ArtBox:
Rotation: 0
Annotations: 0
```

Note that the format for boxes is minimum x, minimum y, maximum x, maximum y. Add -in, -cm or mm to print boxes in inches, centimetres, or millimetres instead of points. Using -page-info-json we can get the information in JSON format. For example:

```
[
  {
    "Page": 1,
    "Label": "i",
    "MediaBox": [ 0.0, 0.0, 600.0, 450.0 ],
    "CropBox": [ 200.0, 200.0, 500.0, 500.0 ],
```

```
      "BleedBox": null,
      "TrimBox": null,
      "ArtBox": null,
      "Rotation": 0,
      "Annotations": 0
   }
]
```

The -pages operation prints the number of pages in the file.

```
cpdf -pages Archos.pdf
8
```

11.2   Setting Document Information

The *document information dictionary* in a PDF file specifies various pieces of information about a PDF. These can be consulted in a PDF viewer (for instance, Acrobat).

Here is a summary of the commands for setting entries in the document information dictionary:

Information	Example command-line fragment
Title	cpdf -set-title "Discourses"
Author	cpdf -set-author "Joe Smith"
Subject	cpdf -set-subject "Behavior"
Keywords	cpdf -set-keywords "Ape Primate"
Creator	cpdf -set-creator "Original Program"
Producer	cpdf -set-producer "Distilling Program"
Creation Date	cpdf -set-create "D:19970915110347-08'00'"
Modification Date	cpdf -set-modify "D:19970915110347-08'00'"
Mark as Trapped	cpdf -set-trapped
Mark as Untrapped	cpdf -set-untrapped

(The details of the format for creation and modification dates can be found in Appendix A. Using the date "now" uses the time and date at which the command is executed. Note also that -producer and -creator may be used to set the producer and/or the creator when writing any file, separate from the operations described in this chapter.)

For example, to set the title, the full command line would be

```
cpdf -set-title "A Night in London" in.pdf -o out.pdf
```

The text string is considered to be in UTF8 format, unless the −raw option is added—in which case, it is unprocessed, save for the replacement of any octal escape sequence such as \017, which is replaced by a character of its value (here, 15).

To set also any field in the XMP metadata, add −also−set−xmp. The field must exist already. To set only the field (not the document information dictionary), add −just−set−xmp instead.

To delete existing non-XMP metadata in line with PDF 2.0, use −remove−dict−entry "/Info" as described in chapter 20.

11.3 XMP Metadata

PDF files can contain a piece of arbitrary metadata, often in XMP format. This is typically stored in an uncompressed stream, so that other applications can read it without having to decode the whole PDF. To set the metadata:

```
cpdf -set-metadata data.xml in.pdf -o out.pdf
```

To remove any metadata:

```
cpdf -remove-metadata in.pdf -o out.pdf
```

To print the current metadata to standard output:

```
cpdf -print-metadata in.pdf
```

To create XMP metadata from scratch, using any information in the Document Information Dictionary (old-style metadata):

```
cpdf -create-metadata in.pdf -o out.pdf
```

To set the XMP metadata date field, use:

```
cpdf -set-metadata-date <date> in.pdf -o out.pdf
```

The date format is defined in Appendix A.2. Using the date "now" uses the time and date at which the command is executed.

11.4 Upon Opening a Document

A mark can be put in a PDF to set the page viewing characteristics upon opening.

NB: If the file has a valid /OpenAction setting, which tells the PDF reader to open at a certain page or position on a page, this can override the page layout or display options described below. To prevent this, preprocess the file with the -remove-dict-entry functionality from Section 20.9:

```
cpdf -remove-dict-entry /OpenAction in.pdf -o out.pdf
```

You can see if the file has such an open action by referring to the output of -info.

NB: The initial view displayed by the dialog box File → Properties → Initial View in Adobe Reader / Acrobat may not reflect exactly the options here. The options here set the flags within the PDF - Adobe products may show different wording.

11.4.1   Page Layout

The -set-page-layout operation specifies the page layout to be used when a document is opened in, for instance, Acrobat. The possible (case-sensitive) values are:

SinglePage	Display one page at a time
OneColumn	Display the pages in one column
TwoColumnLeft	Display the pages in two columns, odd numbered pages on the left
TwoColumnRight	Display the pages in two columns, even numbered pages on the left
TwoPageLeft	(PDF 1.5 and above) Display the pages two at a time, odd numbered pages on the left
TwoPageRight	(PDF 1.5 and above) Display the pages two at a time, even numbered pages on the left

For instance:

```
cpdf -set-page-layout TwoColumnRight in.pdf -o out.pdf
```

11.4.2   Page Mode

The *page mode* in a PDF file defines how a viewer should display the document when first opened. The possible (case-sensitive) values are:

UseNone	Neither document outline nor thumbnail images visible
UseOutlines	Document outline (bookmarks) visible
UseThumbs	Thumbnail images visible
FullScreen	Full-screen mode (no menu bar, window controls, or anything but the document visible)
UseOC	(PDF 1.5 and above) Optional content group panel visible
UseAttachments	(PDF 1.5 and above) Attachments panel visible

For instance:

```
cpdf -set-page-mode FullScreen in.pdf -o out.pdf
```

If full screen mode is selected for document opening, we can also set a mode to be used when the user exits from full-screen mode:

```
cpdf -set-non-full-screen-page-mode UseAttachments in.pdf -o out.pdf
```

As would be expected, FullScreen is not allowed here.

11.4.3   Display Options

The appearance of the PDF viewer upon opening a document may be set with these options. Each is boolean - supply true or false:

-hide-toolbar	Hide the viewer's toolbar
-hide-menubar	Document outline (bookmarks) visible
-hide-window-ui	Hide the viewer's scroll bars
-fit-window	Resize the document's windows to fit size of first page
-center-window	Position the document window in the center of the screen
-display-doc-title	Display the document title instead of the file name in the title bar

For instance:

```
cpdf -hide-toolbar true in.pdf -o out.pdf
```

The page a PDF file opens at can be set using -open-at-page:

```
cpdf -open-at-page 15 in.pdf -o out.pdf
```

To have that page scaled to fit the window in the viewer, use -open-at-page-fit instead:

```
cpdf -open-at-page-fit end in.pdf -o out.pdf
```

(Here, we used `end` to open at the last page. Any page specification describing a single page is ok here.)

Alternatively, we may specify a full destination, of the kind described on page 28:

```
cpdf -open-at-page-custom "[3 /FitR 100 100 300 300]" in.pdf -o out.pdf
```

11.5   Document Language

The document language may be set by giving an IETF BCP 47 language tag:

```
cpdf -set-language "en-GB" in.pdf -o out.pdf
```

This is the top-level language tag. Existing tags on individual parts of the document are preserved.

11.6   Page Labels

It is possible to add *page labels* to a document. These are not the printed on the page, but may be displayed alongside thumbnails or in print dialogue boxes by PDF readers. We use `-add-page-labels` to do this, by default with decimal arabic numbers (1,2,3...). We can add `-label-style` to choose what type of labels to add from these kinds:

`DecimalArabic`	1, 2, 3, 4, 5...
`LowercaseRoman`	i, ii, iii, iv, v...
`UppercaseRoman`	I, II, III, IV, V...
`LowercaseLetters`	a, b, c, ..., z, aa, bb...
`UppercaseLetters`	A, B, C, ..., Z, AA, BB...
`NoLabelPrefixOnly`	No number, but a prefix will be used if defined.

We can use `-label-prefix` to add a textual prefix to each label. Consider a file with twenty pages and no current page labels (a PDF reader will assume 1,2,3...if there are none). We will add the following page labels:

i, ii, iii, iv, 1, 2, 3, 4, 5, 6, 7, 8, 9, 10, A-0, A-1, A-2, A-3, A-4, A-5

Here are the commands, in order:

```
cpdf -add-page-labels in.pdf 1-4 -label-style LowercaseRoman
    -o out.pdf

cpdf -add-page-labels out.pdf 5-14 -o out2.pdf

cpdf -add-page-labels out2.pdf 15-20 -label-prefix "A-"
    -label-startval 0 -o out3.pdf
```

By default the labels begin at page number 1 for each range. To override this, we can use
-label-startval (we used 0 in the final command), where we want the numbers to begin
at zero rather than one. The option -labels-progress can be added to make sure the
start value progresses between sub-ranges when the page range specified is disjoint, e.g 1-9,
30-40 or odd.

Page labels may be removed altogether by using -remove-page-labels command. To
print the page labels from an existing file, use -print-page-labels. For example:

```
$ cpdf -print-page-labels in.pdf
labelstyle: LowercaseRoman
labelprefix: None
startpage: 1
startvalue: 1
labelstyle: DecimalArabic
labelprefix: A
startpage: 9
startvalue: 1
```

Or, in JSON format with -print-page-labels-json:

```
[
  {
    "labelstyle": "LowercaseRoman",
    "labelprefix": null,
    "startpage": 1,
    "startvalue": 1
  },
  {
    "labelstyle": "DecimalArabic",
    "labelprefix": "A",
    "startpage": 9,
    "startvalue": 1
  }
]
```

11.7 Composition of a PDF

The -composition and -composition-json operations show how much space in a PDF is used by each kind of data. Here is the output of -composition for this manual:

```
$ cpdf -composition cpdfmanual.pdf
Images: 0 bytes (0.00%)
Fonts: 144731 bytes (46.72%)
Content streams: 132767 bytes (42.85%)
Structure Info: 0 bytes (0.00%)
Attached Files: 0 bytes (0.00%)
XRef Table: 21082 bytes (6.80%)
Piece Info: 0 bytes (0.00%)
Unclassified: 11229 bytes (3.62%)
```

And here it is in JSON format:

```
$ cpdf -composition-json cpdfmanual.pdf
[
  ["Images", 0, 0.0],
  ["Fonts", 144731, 46.71620256351494],
  ["Content streams", 132767, 42.854468398271194],
  ["Structure Info", 0, 0.0],
  ["Attached Files", 0, 0.0],
  ["XRef Table", 21082, 6.8048378194306816],
  ["Piece Info", 0, 0.0],
  ["Unclassified", 11229, 3.6244912187831857]
]
```

Note that, due to small inaccuracies in the method, it is possible for the Unclassified numbers to be negative.

Chapter 12

File Attachments

```
cpdf -attach-file <filename> [-to-page <page number>] in.pdf -o out.pdf

cpdf -list-attached-files in.pdf

cpdf -remove-files in.pdf -o out.pdf

cpdf -dump-attachments in.pdf -o <directory>
```

PDF supports adding attachments (files of any kind, including other PDFs) to an existing file. The Cpdf tool supports adding and removing *document-level attachments* — that is, ones which are associated with the document as a whole rather than with an individual page, and also *page-level attachments*, associated with a particular page.

12.1 Adding Attachments

To add an attachment, use the -attach-file operation. For instance,

```
cpdf -attach-file sheet.xls in.pdf -o out.pdf
```

attaches the Excel spreadsheet sheet.xls to the input file. If the file already has attachments, the new file is added to their number. You can specify multiple files to be attached by using -attach-file multiple times. They will be attached in the given order.

The -to-page option can be used to specify that the files will be attached to the given page, rather than at the document level. The -to-page option may be specified at most once.

12.2 Listing Attachments

To list all document- and page-level attachments, use the -list-attached-files operation. The page number and filename of each attachment is given, page 0 representing a document-level attachment.

```
$cpdf -list-attached-files 14psfonts.pdf
0 utility.ml
0 utility.mli
4 notes.xls
```

12.3   Removing Attachments

To remove all document-level and page-level attachments from a file, use the -remove-files operation:

```
cpdf -remove-files in.pdf -o out.pdf
```

12.4   Dumping Attachments to File

The -dump-attachments operation, when given a PDF file and a directory path as the output, will write each attachment under its filename (as displayed by -list-attached-files to that directory. The directory must exist prior to the call.

```
cpdf -dump-attachments in.pdf -o /home/fred/attachments
```

Unless either the -raw or -utf8 option is given, the filenames are stripped of dubious special characters before writing. It is converted from unicode to 7 bit ASCII, and the following characters are removed, in addition to any character with ASCII code less than 32:

```
                    / ? < > \ : * | " ^ + =
```

Chapter 13

Images

```
cpdf -extract-images in.pdf [<range>] [-im <path>] [-p2p <path>]
     [-dedup | -dedup-perpage] [-raw] -o <path>

cpdf -list-images[-json] in.pdf [<range>]

cpdf -image-resolution[-json] <minimum resolution> in.pdf [<range>]

cpdf -list-images-used[-json] in.pdf [<range>]

cpdf -process-images [-process-images-info] in.pdf [<range>]
     [-im <filename>] [-jbig2enc <filename>]
     [-lossless-resample[-dpi] <n> | -lossless-to-jpeg <n>]
     [-jpeg-to-jpeg <n>] [-jpeg-to-jpeg-scale <n>]
     [-jpeg-to-jpeg-dpi <n>] [-1bpp-method <method>]
     [-jbig2-lossy-threshold <n>] [-pixel-threshold <n>]
     [-length-threshold <n>] [-percentage-threshold <n>]
     [-dpi-threshold <n>] [-resample-interpolate]
     -o out.pdf

cpdf -rasterize in.pdf <range> -o out.pdf
     [-rasterize[-gray|-1bpp|-jpeg|-jpeggray]
     [-rasterize-res <n>] [-rasterize-jpeg-quality <n>]
     [-rasterize-no-antialias | -rasterize-downsample]
     [-rasterize-annots]

cpdf -output-image in.pdf <range> -o <format>
     [-rasterize[-gray|-1bpp|-jpeg|-jpeggray]
     [-rasterize-res <n>] [-rasterize-jpeg-quality <n>]
     [-rasterize-no-antialias | -rasterize-downsample]
     [-rasterize-annots] [-tobox <BoxName>]
```

13.1 Extracting images

Cpdf can extract the raster images to a given location. JPEG and JPEG2000 and lossless JBIG2 images are extracted directly.

Lossy JBIG2 images are extracted likewise, but an extra __<n> is added, giving the number of the JBIG2Global stream for this image, which is extracted as <n>.jbig2global. You may reconstruct the individual images with, for example, jbig2dec.

Other images are written as PNGs, processed with either ImageMagick's "magick" command, or NetPBM's "pnmtopng" program, whichever is installed.

```
cpdf -extract-images in.pdf [<range>] [-im <path>] [-p2p <path]
     [-dedup | -dedup-perpage] -o <path>
```

The -im or -p2p option is used to give the path to the external tool, one of which must be installed (unless -raw is added, which outputs instead just JPEG or plain .pnm files).

The output specifier, e.g -o output/%%% gives the number format for numbering the images. Output files are named serially from 0, and include the page number too. For example, output files might be called output/000-p1.jpg, output/001-p1.png, output/002-p3.jpg etc. Here is an example invocation:

```
cpdf -extract-images in.pdf -im magick -o output/%%%
```

The output directory must already exist. The -dedup option deduplicates images entirely; the -dedup-perpage option only per page.

13.2   Listing images

The -list-images operation lists all images in the file:

```
6, 1, /Z_Im0, 3300, 2550, 13432, 1, /DeviceGray, /CCITTFaxDecode
9, 2 13 14 15, /Z_Im0, 3376, 2649, 37972, 1, /DeviceGray, /CCITTFaxDecode
```

The fields are *object number, page numbers, image name, width, height, size in bytes, bits per pixel, colour space, filter (compression method)*. With -list-images-json, the same information is available in JSON format:

```
[
  {
    "Object": 6,
    "Pages": [ 1 ],
    "Name": "/Z_Im0",
    "Width": 3300,
    "Height": 2550,
    "Bytes": 13432,
```

```
      "BitsPerComponent": 1,
      "Colourspace": "/DeviceGray",
      "Filter": "/CCITTFaxDecode"
   },
   {
      "Object": 9,
      "Pages": [ 2, 13, 14, 15 ],
      "Name": "/Z_Im0",
      "Width": 3376,
      "Height": 2649,
      "Bytes": 37972,
      "BitsPerComponent": 1,
      "Colourspace": "/DeviceGray",
      "Filter": "/CCITTFaxDecode"
   }
]
```

13.3   Listing images at point of use

To list all images in the given range of pages which fall below a given resolution (in dots-per-inch), use the -image-resolution function:

```
cpdf -image-resolution 300 in.pdf [<range>]
```

Here is the result:

```
2, /Im5, 531, 684, 149.935297, 150.138267, 31
2, /Im6, 184, 164, 149.999988, 150.458710, 39
2, /Im7, 171, 156, 149.999996, 150.579145, 40
2, /Im9, 65, 91, 149.999986, 151.071856, 57
2, /Im10, 94, 60, 149.999990, 152.284285, 59
2, /Im15, 184, 139, 149.960011, 150.672060, 91
4, /Im29, 53, 48, 149.970749, 151.616446, 93
```

The format is *page number, image name, x pixels, y pixels, x resolution, y resolution, object number.* The resolutions refer to the image's effective resolution at point of use (taking account of scaling, rotation etc).

The information is also available in JSON format:

```
[
  {
    "Object": 240,
    "Page": 79,
    "XObject": "/Z_Im0",
    "W": 3326,
    "H": 2584,
    "Xdpi": 300.0,
    "Ydpi": 300.0
  },
  {
    "Object": 243,
    "Page": 80,
    "XObject": "/Z_Im0",
    "W": 3300,
    "H": 2550,
    "Xdpi": 300.0,
    "Ydpi": 300.0
  }
]
```

To list all images regardless of resolution, use -list-images-used or -list-images-used-json instead.

13.4   Removing an Image

To remove a particular image, find its name using -list-images then apply the -draft and -draft-remove-only operations from Section 20.1.

13.5   Processing Images

Cpdf can process images within a PDF, replacing the original with the processed version. It does this by saving out the image data, putting it through an external process, and then reading it back in and re-inserting it. This is typically used to reduce the size of image data, and thus the size of the PDF.

There are a number of option to deal with lossy (e.g JPEG) and lossless images, one or more of which is specified. For example, the -jpeg-to-jpeg option processes existing JPEG images to a given JPEG quality level:

```
cpdf -process-images -im magick -jpeg-to-jpeg 65 in.pdf -o out.pdf
```

ImageMagick is required. Use -im to supply it. If we specify -process-images-info too, we can see the work being done:

```
cpdf -process-images -process-images-info -jpeg-to-jpeg 65
    -im magick in.pdf -o out.pdf
```

Here is sample output:

```
(20/344)  Object 265 (JPEG)... JPEG to JPEG 40798 -> 33463 (82%)
(38/344)  Object 278 (JPEG)... JPEG to JPEG 4382 -> 3482 (79%)
(87/344)  Object 266 (JPEG)... JPEG to JPEG 37227 -> 30199 (81%)
(243/344) Object 209 (JPEG)... no size reduction
(246/344) Object 270 (JPEG)... JPEG to JPEG 202568 -> 191175 (94%)
(281/344) Object 280 (JPEG)... JPEG to JPEG 12255 -> 9825 (80%)
(312/344) Object 279 (JPEG)... JPEG to JPEG 4117 -> 3157 (76%)
```

Similar output appears for the other methods, when they are specified. You can see the counter of work being done, and the result for each image chosen for processing.

The -lossless-to-jpeg option converts lossless images within PDFs to JPEG too, at the given quality level. It may be specified in addition to -jpeg-to-jpeg:

```
cpdf -process-images -jpeg-to-jpeg 65 -lossless-to-jpeg 80
    -im magick in.pdf -o out.pdf
```

Images are only processed if they meet certain thresholds. Changes to the default thresholds may be specified:

Option	Effect	Default value
-pixel-threshold	Images below this number of pixels not processed	25
-length-threshold	Images with less than this number of bytes of data not processed	100
-percentage-threshold	Results not below this percentage of original size discarded	99
-dpi-threshold	Only images above this threshold at all use points processed	(no dpi check)

Instead of compressing lossless images with lossy JPEG compression, we can resample losslessly:

```
cpdf -process-images -im magick -lossless-resample 80 in.pdf -o out.pdf
```

This will resample losslessly-compressed images to be 80 percent of the original width and height. By default, there will be no interpolation. To use interpolation, which may result in slightly larger data, add -resample-interpolate. To use a DPI target instead, use -lossless-resample-dpi instead:

```
cpdf -process-images -im magick -lossless-resample-dpi 300
     in.pdf -o out.pdf
```

We can also use resampling with `-jpeg-to-jpeg`, buy specifying `-jpeg-to-jpeg-scale`:

```
cpdf -process-images -im magick -jpeg-to-jpeg 70 -jpeg-to-jpeg-scale 50
     in.pdf -o out.pdf
```

We can alternatively use a DPI target:

```
cpdf -process-images -im magick -jpeg-to-jpeg 70 -jpeg-to-jpeg-dpi 150
     in.pdf -o out.pdf
```

The methods so far introduced do not operate on 1 bit per pixel data. Different compression mechanisms are typically in use, and we need a different approach. The `-1bpp-method` option specifies what to do with losslessly compressed 1 bit-per-pixel images.

Method	Effect
JBIG2	Lossless JBIG2
JBIG2Lossy	Lossy JBIG2, sharing JBIG2Globals data amongst all images.

These options require the `jbig2enc` program, whose location may be specified with `-jbig2enc`. For lossy JBIG2, the threshold for similarity of data may be set with `-jbig2-lossy-threshold`. For example:

```
cpdf -process-images -jbig2enc jbig2enc -1bpp-method JBIG2Lossy
     -jbig2-lossy-threshold 75 in.pdf -o out.pdf
```

It is not currently possible to reprocess lossless JBIG2 into lossy JBIG2, nor is it possible to recompress into CCITT.

NB: CMYK images will be converted to RGB or untouched by some of these processes. A future version of Cpdf will remove this limitation.

13.6   Rasterization (PDF to image conversion)

Cpdf can send individual pages of a PDF out to `gs` to rasterize them - they are then read back in and replace the original page content:

```
cpdf -gs gs -rasterize in.pdf -o out.pdf
```

Other metadata (for example, bookmarks) is preserved. By default, the resolution is 144dpi, and the raster data is losslessly compressed. It is the Crop Box which is rasterized, or the Media Box if absent. The following options may be added:

Option	Effect
-rasterize-gray	Use grayscale instead of colour
-rasterize-1bpp	Use monochrome instead of colour
-rasterize-jpeg	Use JPEG instead of lossless compression
-rasterize-jpeggray	Use grayscale JPEG instead of lossless compression
-rasterize-jpeg-quality	Set JPEG image quality (0..100)
-rasterize-res	Set the resolution
-rasterize-annots	Rasterize annotations instead of retaining
-rasterize-no-antialias	Turn off antialiasing
-rasterize-downsample	Use better but slower antialiasing
-gs-quiet	Don't show gs output

In addition to rasterization of pages, we can export them in PNG or JPEG format, again by the use of gs:

```
cpdf -gs gs -output-image in.pdf 10-end -o image%%%.png
```

This will extract pages 10 onwards to the files image000.png, image001.png and so on. All the options above apply, and in addition we can choose which box is rasterized:

Option	Effect
-tobox	Choose rasterization box

For example:

```
cpdf -gs gs -output-image -tobox /BleedBox -rasterize-jpeg in.pdf
      -o image%%%.jpeg
```

Chapter 14

Fonts

```
cpdf -list-fonts[-json] in.pdf

cpdf -print-font-table <font name> -print-font-table-page <n> in.pdf

cpdf -copy-font fromfile.pdf -copy-font-page <int>
    -copy-font-name <name> in.pdf [<range>] -o out.pdf

cpdf -remove-fonts in.pdf -o out.pdf

cpdf -missing-fonts in.pdf

cpdf -embed-missing-fonts -gs <path to gs> in.pdf -o out.pdf

cpdf -extract-font <page number>,<pdf font name> in.pdf -o out.font
```

14.1 Listing Fonts

The -list-fonts operation prints the fonts in the document, one-per-line to standard output. For example:

```
1 /F245 /Type0 /Cleargothic-Bold /Identity-H
1 /F247 /Type0 /ClearGothicSerialLight /Identity-H
1 /F248 /Type1 /Times-Roman /WinAnsiEncoding
1 /F250 /Type0 /Cleargothic-RegularItalic /Identity-H
2 /F13 /Type0 /Cleargothic-Bold /Identity-H
2 /F16 /Type0 /Arial-ItalicMT /Identity-H
2 /F21 /Type0 /ArialMT /Identity-H
2 /X02 /F58 /Type1 /Times-Roman /WinAnsiEncoding
2 /F59 /Type0 /ClearGothicSerialLight /Identity-H
2 /F61 /Type0 /Cleargothic-BoldItalic /Identity-H
2 /F68 /Type0 /Cleargothic-RegularItalic /Identity-H
3 /F47 /Type0 /Cleargothic-Bold /Identity-H
3 /F49 /Type0 /ClearGothicSerialLight /Identity-H
```

```
3 /F50 /Type1 /Times-Roman /WinAnsiEncoding
3 /F52 /Type0 /Cleargothic-BoldItalic /Identity-H
3 /F54 /Type0 /TimesNewRomanPS-BoldItalicMT /Identity-H
3 /F57 /Type0 /Cleargothic-RegularItalic /Identity-H
4 /F449 /Type0 /Cleargothic-Bold /Identity-H
4 /F451 /Type0 /ClearGothicSerialLight /Identity-H
4 /F452 /Type1 /Times-Roman /WinAnsiEncoding
```

The first column gives the page number, the second the internal unique font name (or, if the font is used in a Form XObject, the path e.g /X1/F0), the third the type of font (Type1, TrueType etc), the fourth the PDF font name, the fifth the PDF font encoding.

The information is also available in JSON format with -list-fonts-json:

```
[
  {
    "page": 1,
    "name": "/F47",
    "subtype": "/Type1",
    "basefont": "/XYPLPB+NimbusSanL-Bold",
    "encoding": null
  },
  {
    "page": 1,
    "name": "/F50",
    "subtype": "/Type0",
    "basefont": "/MCBERL+URWPalladioL-Roma",
    "encoding": "/Identity-H"
  }
]
```

14.2   Listing characters in a font

We can use Cpdf to find out which characters are available in a given font, and to print the map between character codes, unicode codepoints, and Adobe glyph names. This is presently a best-effort service, and does not cover all font/encoding types.

We find the name of the font by using -list-fonts:

```
$ ./cpdf -list-fonts cpdfmanual.pdf 1
1 /F46 /Type1 /XYPLPB+NimbusSanL-Bold
1 /F49 /Type1 /MCBERL+URWPalladioL-Roma
```

We may then print the table, giving either the font's name (e.g /F46) or basename (e.g /XYPLPB+NimbusSanL-Bold):

```
$ ./cpdf -print-font-table /XYPLPB+NimbusSanL-Bold
         -print-font-table-page 1 cpdfmanual.pdf
67 = U+0043 (C - LATIN CAPITAL LETTER C) = /C
68 = U+0044 (D - LATIN CAPITAL LETTER D) = /D
70 = U+0046 (F - LATIN CAPITAL LETTER F) = /F
71 = U+0047 (G - LATIN CAPITAL LETTER G) = /G
76 = U+004C (L - LATIN CAPITAL LETTER L) = /L
80 = U+0050 (P - LATIN CAPITAL LETTER P) = /P
84 = U+0054 (T - LATIN CAPITAL LETTER T) = /T
97 = U+0061 (a - LATIN SMALL LETTER A) = /a
99 = U+0063 (c - LATIN SMALL LETTER C) = /c
100 = U+0064 (d - LATIN SMALL LETTER D) = /d
101 = U+0065 (e - LATIN SMALL LETTER E) = /e
104 = U+0068 (h - LATIN SMALL LETTER H) = /h
105 = U+0069 (i - LATIN SMALL LETTER I) = /i
108 = U+006C (l - LATIN SMALL LETTER L) = /l
109 = U+006D (m - LATIN SMALL LETTER M) = /m
110 = U+006E (n - LATIN SMALL LETTER N) = /n
111 = U+006F (o - LATIN SMALL LETTER O) = /o
112 = U+0070 (p - LATIN SMALL LETTER P) = /p
114 = U+0072 (r - LATIN SMALL LETTER R) = /r
115 = U+0073 (s - LATIN SMALL LETTER S) = /s
116 = U+0074 (t - LATIN SMALL LETTER T) = /t
```

The first column is the character code, the second the Unicode codepoint, the character itself and its Unicode name, and the third the Adobe glyph name.

14.3 Copying Fonts

In order to use a font other than the standard 14 with -add-text, it must be added to the file. The font source PDF is given, together with the font's resource name on a given page, and that font is copied to all the pages in the input file's range, and then written to the output file.

The font is named in the output file with its basefont name, so it can be easily used with -add-text.

For example, if the file fromfile.pdf has a font /GHLIGA+c128 with the name /F10 on page 1 (this information can be found with -list-fonts), the following would copy the font to the file in.pdf on all pages, writing the output to out.pdf:

```
cpdf -copy-font fromfile.pdf -copy-font-name /F10
     -copy-font-page 1 in.pdf -o out.pdf
```

Text in this font can then be added by giving -font /GHLIGA+c128. Be aware that due to the vagaries of PDF font handling concerning which characters are present in the source font, not all characters may be available, or Cpdf may not be able to work out the conversion from UTF8 to the font's own encoding. You may add -raw to the command line to avoid any conversion, but the encoding (mapping from input codes to glyphs) may be non-obvious and require knowledge of the PDF format to divine.

14.4   Removing Fonts

To remove embedded fonts from a document, use -remove-fonts. PDF readers will substitute
local fonts for the missing fonts. The use of this function is only recommended when file size is
the sole consideration.

```
cpdf -remove-fonts in.pdf -o out.pdf
```

14.5   Missing Fonts

The -missing-fonts operation lists any unembedded fonts in the document, one per line.

```
cpdf -missing-fonts in.pdf
```

The format is

```
Page number, Name, Subtype, Basefont, Encoding
```

The operation -embed-missing-fonts will process the file with gs (which must be installed)
to embed missing fonts (where found):

```
cpdf -embed-missing-fonts -gs gs in.pdf -o out.pdf
```

*Note: putting a PDF file through gs in this manner may not be lossless: some metadata may not be
preserved.*

14.6   Extracting Fonts

We may extract a font file by giving the page number and the PDF font resource name, as
printed by -list-fonts or -list-fonts-json. For example, for the TrueType font /F50
on page 5:

```
cpdf -extract-font 5,/F50 in.pdf -o out.ttf
```

Chapter 15

PDF and JSON

```
cpdf in.pdf -output-json -o out.json
      [-output-json-parse-content-streams]
      [-output-json-no-stream-data]
      [-output-json-decompress-streams]
      [-output-json-clean-strings]
      [-utf8]
cpdf -j in.json -o out.pdf
```

In addition to reading and writing PDF files in the original Adobe format, Cpdf can read and write them in its own CPDFJSON format, for somewhat easier extraction of information, modification of PDF files, and so on.

15.1 Converting PDF to JSON

We convert a PDF file to JSON format like this:

```
cpdf -output-json in.pdf -o out.json
```

The resultant JSON file is an array of arrays containing an object number followed by an object, one for each object in the file and two special ones:

- Object -1: Cpdf's own data with the PDF version number, CPDF JSON format number, and flags used when writing (which may be required when reading):

  - /CPDFJSONformatversion (CPDFJSON integer (see below), currently 3)

  - /CPDFJSONcontentparsed (boolean, true if content streams have been parsed)

  - /CPDFJSONstreamdataincluded (boolean, true if stream data included. Cannot round-trip if false).

77

- /CPDFJSONmajorpdfversion (CPDFJSON integer)
- /CPDFJSONminorpdfversion (CPDFJSON integer)

- Object 0: The PDF's trailer dictionary
- Objects 1..n: The PDF's objects.

Objects are formatted thus:

- PDF arrays, dictionaries, booleans, and strings are the same as in JSON.
- Integers are written as {"I": 0}
- Floats are written as {"F": 0.0}
- Names are written as {"N": "/Pages"}
- Indirect references are integers
- Streams are {"S": [dict, data]}
- Strings are converted to JSON string format in a way which, when reversed, results in the original string. For best results when editing files, use the -utf8 option. The string representation is again reversible, but easier to edit. Unicode strings are written as {"U": "the text"}.

Here is an example of the output for a small PDF:

```
[
  [
    -1,
    { "/CPDFJSONformatversion": { "I": 2 },
      "/CPDFJSONcontentparsed": false,
      "/CPDFJSONstreamdataincluded": true,
      "/CPDFJSONmajorpdfversion": { "I": 1 },
      "/CPDFJSONminorpdfversion": { "I": 1 } }
  ],
  [
    0,
    { "/Size": { "I": 4 }, "/Root": 4,
      "/ID" : [ <elided>, <elided>] } ],
  [
    1, { "/Type": { "N": "/Pages" }, "/Kids": [ 3 ], "/Count": { "I": 1 } }
  ],
  [
    2,
    {"S": [{ "/Length": { "I": 49 } },
     "1 0 0 1 50 770 cm BT/F0 36 Tf(Hello, World!)Tj ET"] }
  ],
  [
    3, { "/Type": { "N": "/Page" }, "/Parent": 1,
    "/Resources": {
```

```
      "/Font": {
        "/F0": {
          "/Type": { "N": "/Font" },
          "/Subtype": { "N": "/Type1" },
          "/BaseFont": { "N": "/Times-Italic" }
        }
      }
    },
    "/MediaBox":
      [{ "I": 0 }, { "I": 0 },
        { "F": 595.2755905510001 }, { "F": 841.88976378 }],
    "/Rotate": { "I": 0 },
    "/Contents": [ 2 ] } ],
[
  4, { "/Type": { "N": "/Catalog" }, "/Pages": 1 } ]
]
```

The option -output-json-parse-content-streams will also convert content streams to JSON, so our example content stream will be expanded:

```
2, {
"S": [
  {}, [
  [
  { "F": 1.0 }, { "F": 0.0 }, { "F": 0.0 }, { "F": 1.0 }, { "F": 50.0 }, {
  "F": 770.0 }, "cm" ], [ "BT" ], [ "/F0", { "F": 36.0 }, "Tf" ], [
  "Hello, World!", "Tj" ], [ "ET" ] ]
] } ]
```

The option -output-json-no-stream-data simply elides the stream data instead, leading to much smaller JSON files. But these may not be round-tripped back into PDF, of course.

The option -output-json-decompress-streams keeps the streams intact, and decompresses them.

The option -output-json-clean-strings converts any UTF16BE strings with no high bytes to PDFDocEncoding prior to output, so that editing them is easier. *Note: this is deprecated as of version 2.6 in favour of* -utf8.

15.2   Converting JSON to PDF

We can load a JSON PDF file with the -j option in place of a PDF file anywhere in a normal Cpdf command. A range may be applied, just like any other file.

```
cpdf -j in.json -o out.pdf
```

It is not required that /Length entries in CPDFJSON stream dictionaries be correctly updated when the JSON file is edited: Cpdf will fix them when loading.

Chapter 16

Optional Content Groups

```
cpdf -ocg-list in.pdf
cpdf -ocg-rename -ocg-rename-from <a> -ocg-rename-to <b> in.pdf -o out.pdf
cpdf -ocg-order-all in.pdf -o out.pdf
cpdf -ocg-coalesce-on-name in.pdf -o out.pdf
```

In a PDF file, optional content groups are used to group graphical elements together, so they may appear or not, depending on the preference of the user. They are similar in some ways to layers in graphics illustration programs.

```
cpdf -ocg-list in.pdf
```

List the optional content groups in the PDF, one per line, to standard output. UTF8.

```
cpdf -ocg-rename -ocg-rename-from <a> -ocg-rename-to <b> in.pdf -o out.pdf
```

Rename an optional content group.

```
cpdf -ocg-coalesce-on-name in.pdf -o out.pdf
```

Coalesce optional content groups. For example, if we merge or stamp two files both with an OCG called "Layer 1", we will have two different optional content groups. Running -ocg-coalesce-on-name will merge the two into a single optional content group.

```
cpdf -ocg-order-all in.pdf -o out.pdf
```

Ensure that every optional content group appears in the order list.

Chapter 17

Creating New PDFs

```
cpdf -create-pdf [-create-pdf-pages <n>]
    [-create-pdf-papersize <paper size>] -o out.pdf

cpdf -typeset <text file> [-create-pdf-papersize <size>]
    [-font <font>] [-font-size <size>]
    [-subformat <subformat>] [-title <string>] -o out.pdf

cpdf -jpeg <filename> [-subformat <subformat>] [-title <string>]
    -o out.pdf

cpdf -png <filename> [-subformat <subformat>] [-title <string>]
    -o out.pdf

cpdf -jpeg2000 <filename> [-subformat <subformat>] [-title <string>]
    -o out.pdf

cpdf [-jbig2-global <filename>] -jbig2 <filename>
    [-jbig2-global | -jbig2-global-clear]
    [-jbig2 <filename>] ...
    [-subformat <subformat>] [-title <string>] -o out.pdf
```

17.1   A new blank PDF

We can build a new PDF file, given a number of pages and a paper size. The default is one page, A4 portrait.

```
cpdf -create-pdf -create-pdf-pages 20
    -create-pdf-papersize usletterportrait -o out.pdf
```

The standard paper sizes are listed in Section 3.1, or you may specify the width and height directly, as described in the same chapter.

17.2   Convert a text file to PDF

A basic text to PDF convertor is included in Cpdf. It takes a UTF8 text file (ASCII is a subset of UTF8) and typesets it ragged-right, splitting on whitespace. Both Windows and Unix line endings are allowed.

```
cpdf -typeset file.txt -create-pdf-papersize a3portrait
    -font Courier -font-size 10 -o out.pdf
```

The standard paper sizes are listed in Section 3.1, or you may specify the width and height directly, as described in the same chapter. The font may be specified as described in Section 8.2.5. The default font is Times-Roman and the default size is 12.

To produce a PDF in PDF/UA-1 or PDF/UA-2 format add, say, -subformat PDF/UA-2 -title "Thesis" to the command line.

17.3   Make a PDF from a PNG, JPEG or JPEG2000 image

Simple facilities for making PDFs from PNG and JPEG images are included in Cpdf. The resulting file can be written out, or used for further operations.

For PNG files, the file must have no transparency and no interlacing, and must not be palletised:

```
cpdf -png image.png -o out.pdf
cpdf image.png AND -add-text "My Image" -o out.pdf
```

Notice that the -png can be omitted if your file has a standard file extension. Almost any JPEG file may be used with -jpeg or again, with a -jpg or -jpeg extension:

```
cpdf -jpeg image.jpg -o out.pdf
```

JPEG2000 images may be used similarly, with -jpeg2000 or alone with a jp2, jpx or jpf extension:

```
cpdf -jpeg2000 image.jp2 -o out.pdf
```

The output file will have one point of width or height for each pixel in the input.

To produce a PDF in PDF/UA-1 or PDF/UA-2 format add, say, -subformat PDF/UA-2 -title "Opus" to the command line.

17.4   Make a PDF from one or more JBIG2 images

Cpdf can build multi-pages files from one or more PDF-appropriate JBIG2 fragments, prepared by the jbig2enc program. In lossless mode, there is one JBIG2 fragment for each page:

```
cpdf -jbig2 1.jbig2 -jbig2 2.jbig2 -jbig2 3.jbig2 -o out.pdf
```

This produces a PDF of three pages. In lossy mode, a JBIG2Globals stream can be added, which contains shared data for several pages:

```
cpdf -jbig2-global 0.jbig2globals
     -jbig2 1.jbig2 -jbig2 2.jbig2 -jbig2 3.jbig2 -o out.pdf
```

The -jbig2-global option may be used to change the JBIG2Globals stream in use. The -jbig2-global-clear option may be used to cease use of a globals stream and return to lossless mode.

To produce a PDF in PDF/UA-1 or PDF/UA-2 format add, say, -subformat PDF/UA-2 -title "Opus" to the command line.

Chapter 18

Drawing on PDFs

```
cpdf in.pdf [<range>] -draw <draw operations> [-underneath] -o out.pdf
cpdf -text-width <text> [-font <font>] [-fontsize <fontsize>]
```

BUILDING AND SHOWING PATHS
-rect Draw rectangle
-to Move to
-line Add line to path
-bez Add Bezier curve to path
-bez23 Add Bezier curve to path
-bez13 Add Bezier curve to path
-circle Add circle to path
-stroke Stroke path
-fill Fill path
-filleo Fill path, even odd
-strokefill Stroke and fill path
-strokefilleo Stroke and fill path, even odd
-close Close path

CLIPPING WITH PATHS
-clip Clip
-clipeo Clip, even odd

PATH PARAMETERS
-strokecol Set stroke colour
-fillcol Set fill colour
-thick Set stroke thickness
-cap Set cap
-join Set join
-miter Set miter limit
-dash Set dash pattern

THE GRAPHICS STACK AND MATRICES
-push Push graphics stack
-pop Pop graphics stack
-matrix Append to graphics matrix
-mtrans Translate the graphics matrix
-mrot Rotate the graphics matrix
-mscale Scale the graphics matrix
-mshearx Shear the graphics matrix in X
-msheary Shear the graphics matrix in Y

RE-USE WITH XOBJECTS
-xobj-bbox Specify the bounding box for xobjects
-xobj Begin saving a sequence of graphics operators
-end-xobj End saving a sequence of graphics operators
-use Use a saved sequence of graphics operators

IMAGES
-draw-jpeg Load a JPEG from file and name it
-draw-png Load a PNG from file and name it
-image Draw an image which has already been loaded

TRANSPARENCY
-fill-opacity Set opacity
-stroke-opacity Set stroke opacity

TEXT
-bt Begin text
-et End text
-text Draw text
-stext Draw text with %specials
-para Typeset a paragraph
-paras Typeset multiple paragraphs
-leading Set leading
-charspace Set character spacing
-wordspace Set word space
-textscale Set text scale
-rendermode Set text rendering mode
-rise Set text rise
-nl New line

THE NEXT PAGE
-newpage Move to a fresh page

STRUCTURE INFORMATION
-draw-struct-tree Add structure information
-tag Begin marked content

```
-end-tag End marked content
-stag Begin structure tree branch
-end-stag End structure tree branch
-auto-tags Automatically tag paragraphs and images
-no-auto-tags Refrain from automatically tagging paragraphs and images
-artifact Begin manual artifact
-end-artifact End manual artifact
-no-auto-artifacts Prevent automatic addition of artifacts during postprocessing
-namespace Set the namespace for future branches of the tree
-eltinfo Set element information
-end-eltinfo Erase element information
-rolemap Set role map
```

18.1   Basics

We can draw on an existing PDF (or a new one created with -create-pdf from the previous
chapter) using the -draw operation. This provides commands for drawing vector graphics,
simple text and adding images. For example:

```
cpdf -create-pdf AND -draw -bt -text Hello -et -o out.pdf
cpdf in.pdf -draw -bt -text Hello -et -o out.pdf
```

The first example builds a new A4 portrait PDF with one page, and writes Hello in the default
12pt Times Roman font at the bottom left. The second does the same, but for every page of an
existing PDF.

18.2   Building and showing paths

```
-rect "x y w h" Draw rectangle
-to "x y" Move to
-line "x y" Add line to path
-bez "x1 y1 x2 y2 x3 y3" Add Bezier curve to path
-bez23 "x2 y2 x3 y3" Add Bezier curve to path
-bez13 "x1 y1 x3 y3" Add Bezier curve to path
-circle "x y r" Add circle to path
-stroke Stroke path
-fill Fill path
-filleo Fill path, even odd
-strokefill Stroke and fill path
-strokefilleo Stroke and fill path, even odd
-close Close path
```

To draw line art, we build paths and then stroke or fill them. For example:

```
cpdf -create-pdf AND -draw -to "100 100" -line "400 400" -stroke
      -line "400 100" -line "100 100" -stroke
      -o out.pdf
```

We use -to to start the path at a given coordinate, -line to extend the path with each line, and then -stroke to stroke the path. Coordinates in a PDF file have the origin $(0, 0)$ at the bottom-left of the page. All units are in points (1/72 inch). This creates the following PDF:

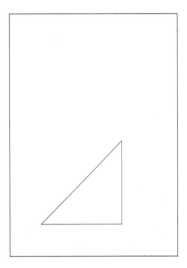

Alternatively, we may use -close to draw the final line back to the starting point:

```
cpdf -create-pdf AND -draw -to "100 100" -line "400 400"
      -line "400 100" -close -stroke
      -o out.pdf
```

We can have multiple such subpaths in a path, by closing and carrying on. We can fill our path with -fill:

```
cpdf -create-pdf AND -draw -to "100 100" -line "400 400"
      -line "400 100" -close -fill
      -o out.pdf
```

Now we have a filled triangle:

The operations -filleo, -strokefill and -strokefilleo provide alternative combinations of stroke, fill, and winding rule.

We can save time when drawing rectangles by using the -rect operation, which takes the lower left coordinate, width and height. There is no need to explicitly close the rectangle.

```
cpdf -create-pdf AND -draw -rect "200 300 200 300" -stroke
    -o out.pdf
```

We can build bezier curves using -bez, -bez23 and -bez13. The first adds a bezier path using six coordinates - for the control points first, and then for the end point (the start point is the current coordinate):

```
cpdf -create-pdf AND -draw -to "100 100" -bez "400 600 600 400 300 300"
    -stroke -o out.pdf
```

Here is the result:

The operation -bez23 is a shorthand used when the first control point is equal to the current point. The operation -bez13 is a shorthand used when the second control point is equal to the final point.

To avoid calculating the Bezier curves for a circle manually, Cpdf can generate them automatically when given the centre and radius:

```
cpdf -create-pdf AND -draw -circle "200 200 100"
    -stroke -o out.pdf
```

18.3   Clipping with paths

```
-clip Clip
-clipeo Clip, even odd
```

We can use a path to form a clipping region for subsequent content using -clip or -clipeo. For example:

```
cpdf -create-pdf AND -draw -circle "300 300 100" -clip
    -circle "300 350 100" -fill -o out.pdf
```

Here is the result:

18.4   Path parameters

```
-strokecol "g" | "r g b" | "c y m k" | <namedcolour> Set stroke colour
-fillcol "g" | "r g b" | "c y m k" | <namedcolour> Set fill colour
-thick <n> Set stroke thickness
-cap butt | round | square Set cap
-join miter | round | bevel Set join
-miter <n> Set miter limit
-dash <pattern> Set dash pattern
```

We can set stroke and fill colours for our paths, either as greyscale (one component), RGB (three components) or CMYK (four components), or by naming a colour as described in Chapter 8:

```
cpdf -create-pdf AND -draw -circle "200 200 100" -thick 20
     -strokecol 0.5 -fillcol "0.2 0.7 0.2" -strokefill -o out.pdf
```

Here is the result:

We can set line caps and joins with -cap, -join:

```
cpdf -create-pdf AND -draw -to "100 100"
     -join round -cap round -thick 40
     -line "200 200" -line "220 100" -stroke
     -o out.pdf
```

Then we see:

The miter limit (see PDF reference for details) may be set with -miter.

Lines may have dash patterns. A dash pattern consists of one or more numbers. All save the last form the list of dash lengths and gap lengths. The last is the phase, which defines how far along the pattern we start. For example, using a dash pattern of "30 20 0" i.e black 30, white 20, phase 0:

```
cpdf -create-pdf AND -draw -to "100 100"
        -dash "30 20 0" -thick 20 -line "400 300" -stroke
        -o out.pdf
```

Here is the result:

18.5   The graphics stack and matrices

```
-push Push graphics stack
-pop Pop graphics stack
-matrix "a b c d e f" Append to graphics matrix
-mtrans "tx ty" Translate the graphics matrix
-mrot "x y a" Rotate the graphics matrix counterclockwise around (x, y) by angle a in radians
-mscale "x y sx sy" Scale the graphics matrix around (x, y)
-mshearx "x y a" Shear the graphics matrix in X around (x, y) by angle a
-msheary "x y a" Shear the graphics matrix in Y around (x, y) by angle a
```

PDF maintains a stack of graphics state, which we can manipulate with -push which stores the current state, then modify the state for our own purposes, and then use -pop to restore the previous state. Such invocations may be nested. Here is a simple example:

```
cpdf -create-pdf AND -draw -circle "200 200 100" -fillcol red -fill
        -push -fillcol blue -circle "300 300 100" -fill
        -pop -circle "400 400 100" -fill  -o out.pdf
```

When we use -pop the colour returns to the saved one:

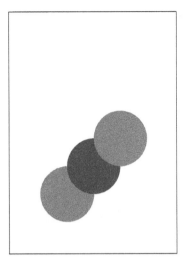

One very common use for a -push/-pop pair is to isolate the effects of an operation which modifies the current transformation matrix. These operations are used to translate, rotate, scale and so on. For example:

```
cpdf -create-pdf AND -draw -circle "200 200 100" -stroke -push
      -mrot "0 0 -0.3" -mscale "0 0 1.5 2" -circle "200 200 100" -stroke
      -pop -circle "200 200 50" -fill -o out.pdf
```

This is the result. See how the graphics transformation is undone when -push is invoked:

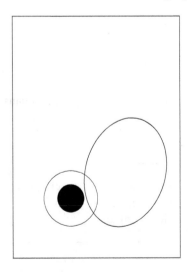

This is important because, in the absence of -push and -pop there would be no way to reverse the effect of a graphics matrix modification except to manually calculate its inverse and apply it.

NB: When writing text (see below) the -font option is not subject to -push and -pop. Text is set the the font most recently chosen on the command line.

18.6   Re-use with XObjects

`-xobj-bbox "x y w h"` Specify the bounding box for xobjects
`-xobj <name>` Begin saving a sequence of graphics operators
`-end-xobj` End saving a sequence of graphics operators
`-use <name>` Use a saved sequence of graphics operators

In our examples, we have sometimes had to write the same operations multiple times. To avoid this, PDF has a mechanism called an XObject. This allows us to save a set of operations for re-use in different contexts, or on different pages. For example, here we store an XObject which just strokes a circle. We then `-use` it once, and alter the colour and transformation matrix and `-use` it again.

```
cpdf -create-pdf AND -draw -xobj-bbox "0 0 200 200" -xobj A
     -circle "100 100 50" -stroke -end-xobj
     -use A -strokecol red -mtrans "20 20" -use A -o out.pdf
```

Note that we must specify a bounding box for the XObject with `-xobj-bbox`. Here is the result:

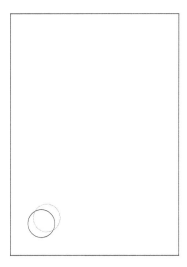

XObjects may be nested.

18.7   Images

`-draw-jpeg <name>=<filename>` Load a JPEG from file and name it
`-draw-png <name>=<filename>` Load a PNG from file and name it
`-image <name>` Draw an image which has already been loaded

We can include a 24bit non-transparent and non-interlaced PNG, or any JPEG by using
-draw-jpeg or -draw-png to load it and assign it a name. We can then use -image to
use it at any point:

```
cpdf -create-pdf AND -draw -draw-png A=sheet.png
     -mscale "0 0 400 294" -image A -o out.pdf
```

Here is the result:

You can see we had to scale by the width and height of the image to draw it at the size we
expect.

18.8   Transparency

```
-fill-opacity <n> Set opacity
-stroke-opacity <n> Set stroke opacity
```

We can set fill and stroke transparencies, between 0 (fully transparent) and 1 (fully opaque):

```
cpdf -create-pdf AND -draw -fill-opacity 0.5
     -circle "250 300 150" -fill -circle "350 300 150" -fill
     -o out.pdf
```

Here is the result:

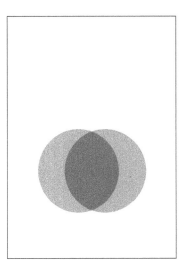

Notice that we used −fill twice, to ensure each circle was in a different path. If they had been part of the same path, the effect would be different.

18.9   Text

```
−bt Begin text
−et End text
−text <text> Draw text
−stext <text> Draw text with %specials
−font <fontname> Set font
−font−size <n> Set font size
−leading <n> Set leading
−charspace <n> Set character spacing
−wordspace <n> Set word space
−textscale <n> Set text scale
−rendermode <n> Set text rendering mode
−rise <n> Set text rise
−nl New line
```

We can draw text in a *text section*, which must start with −bt and end with −et. For example:

```
cpdf −create−pdf AND −draw −mtrans "50 50" −font Helvetica −font−size 144
      −bt −text "Hello" −et −o out.pdf
```

Here is the result:

If we use -stext instead of -text the usual special values from Chapter 8 (with the exception of URL links) may be used:

```
cpdf -create-pdf AND -draw -mtrans "50 50" -font-size 144
     -bt -stext "Page %Page" -et -o out.pdf
```

Now we see:

We can use -text multiple times, interspersing operators which change the text state, such as font and font size:

```
cpdf -create-pdf AND -draw -mtrans "10 20" -font-size 72
     -bt -text "Different " -font Times-BoldItalic -text "fonts"
     -font-size 36 -text " and sizes" -et -o out.pdf
```

Here is the result:

We can alter the character space, word space, horizontal scaling (100 = no scaling, less than 100 shrink, more than 100 stretch), and text rise:

```
cpdf -create-pdf AND -draw -mtrans "10 20" -font-size 72
     -bt -textscale 75 -charspace 5 -wordspace 20 -text "Different "
     -font Times-BoldItalic -text "fonts" -font-size 36 -rise 40
     -text " and sizes" -et -o out.pdf
```

Now we see:

Different *fonts* and sizes

Text may appear on multiple lines. We set up the line spacing with −leading then make new lines with −nl:

```
cpdf -create-pdf AND -draw -mtrans "100 200" -font-size 50
     -leading 55 -bt -text "This is" -nl -text "on multiple"
     -nl -text "lines" -et -o out.pdf
```

Now we have:

This is
on multiple
lines

When composing text, we may need to find the width of a piece of text to see where to break it, or for right alignment. We can use -text-width for this:

```
cpdf -font Times-Roman -font-size 20 -text-width "Hello"
```

The result is in points.

We can change the text rendering mode to show outline text or, in this example, to use text as a clipping region:

```
cpdf -create-pdf AND -draw -rendermode 7 -mtrans "100 200" -font-size 50
     -leading 55 -bt -text "This is" -nl -text "on multiple"
     -nl -text "lines" -et -circle "100 0 100" -fill -o out.pdf
```

Here is the result:

This is
ɔn multip
ˀˢ

Here are the text rendering modes:

    0   Fill text (default)
    1   Stroke text
    2   Fill, then stroke text
    3   Neither fill nor stroke (invisible)
    4   Fill text and add to path for clipping
    5   Stroke text and add to path for clipping
    6   Fill, then stroke text and add to path for clipping
    7   Add text to path for clipping

NB: When writing text the -font option is not subject to -push and -pop. Text is set the the font most recently chosen on the command line.

NB: To use a TrueType font with -draw, the -load-ttf must appear after the -draw.

NB: To use -embed-std14, put it before -draw.

18.10   Paragraphs

We can add a paragraph of text of a given width and justification (Left, Right, or Centre) using the -para operation:

```
cpdf -create-pdf AND -draw -mtrans "200 400" -font-size 20 -leading 25
    -bt -para "L200pt=This is a paragraph of width 100pt, left-justif
    ied, containing more than one line..." -et
    -o out.pdf
```

Notice the paragraph specification L200pt= for left justified, 200pt-wide at the beginning of the string. Notice also we must give a value for -leading. Here is the result:

This is a paragraph of
width 200pt,
left-justified, containing
more than one line...

Multiple paragraphs with optional indenting may be laid out with -paras:

```
cpdf -create-pdf AND -draw -mtrans "200 500" -bt -font-size 20 -leading 25
    -indent 20 -paras "L300=This is the first paragraph, which is spread
    over multiple lines at this width...\nAnd here is the second, also ta
    king more than one line.\nHere is a little one." -et AND -decompress
    -o out.pdf
```

We specify the newlines with \n, and the indentation with -indent. Here is the result.

This is the first paragraph, which is
spread over multiple lines at this
width...
    And here is the second, also
taking more than one line.
    Here is a little one.

Note that there is no automatic typesetting over multiple pages with -paras.

18.11   The next page

```
-newpage Move to a fresh page
```

If the drawing range is a single page, and the next page already exists, the drawing operation
-newpage operation moves to the next page. Otherwise, it creates a fresh page of the same
dimensions as the last page of the document, and sets the drawing range to just that page. For
example:

```
cpdf -create-pdf AND -draw -bt -text "Page 1" -et
     -newpage -bt -text "Page 2" -et
     -o out.pdf
```

This will create a two page PDF with "Page 1" written on page one and "Page 2" written on
page two.

18.12   Structure information

A PDF may contain, in addition to its graphical content, a tree of information concerning the
logical organization of the document into chapters, sections, paragraphs, figures and so on.
When used with a standard set of pre-defined data types, this is known as Tagged PDF. Some
PDF subformats, such as PDF/UA, mandate – amongst other things – the full tagging of the file.
      When drawing, Cpdf can add such structure information. Partly this can happen automati-
cally, partly it is for the user to add the tags. NB: These facilities are presently limited to drawing
new PDFs.
      To enable the generation of structure information, we add -draw-struct-tree to our
command:

```
cpdf -create-pdf AND
     -draw-struct-tree -draw -bt -text "Hello, World" -et -o out.pdf
```

Structure information in a PDF is in the form of a tree. We can now show the structure tree, and
see that our paragraph on page one has been automatically tagged by Cpdf:

```
$cpdf -print-struct-tree out.pdf
StructTreeRoot
└── P (1)
```

To prevent such automatic tagging, relying only on manual tags, use -no-auto-tags. The
effect may be reversed at any point with -auto-tags. Unless told otherwise, Cpdf auto-tags
text added using -text, -stext and -paras with tag P, and images with tag Figure.
      There are two types of tag we can add manually. One kind is used to tag individual pieces
of content. We do this with a -tag/-end-tag pair. Note that nesting is not permitted here.
For example, let us tag a heading:

```
cpdf -create-pdf AND -draw-struct-tree -draw -mtrans "50 700"
     -font-size 40 -no-auto-tags -tag H1 -bt -text "This is the heading"
     -et -end-tag -auto-tags -mtrans "0 -100" -font-size 20 -leading 25
     -bt -paras "L200pt=This is the first paragraph, which spreads over
more than one line\nHere is the second, which also has multiple lines..."
     -et -o out.pdf
```

We turned off auto-tagging with -no-auto-tag, then used -tag H1 and -end-tag to tag the
heading. Then we turned auto-tagging back on with -auto-tag. Here is the result, visually:

And here is the structure tree:

```
StructTreeRoot
├── H1 (1)
├── P (1)
└── P (1)
```

Content tagging is flat - every part of the content of a page is part of only one -tag. The logical
structure of a document, however, is a tree structure – sections contain paragraphs, and so
on. To build the logical structure tree, we add structure tags using -stag / -end-stag pairs
which, of course, may be nested. For example, let's put our H1, and P sections in a Section
structure tag:

```
cpdf -create-pdf AND -draw-struct-tree -draw -mtrans "50 700"
     -font-size 40 -no-auto-tags -stag Section -tag H1 -bt
     -text "This is the heading" -et -end-tag -auto-tags -mtrans "0 -100"
     -font-size 20 -leading 25 -bt -paras "L200pt=This is the first parag
raph, which spreads over more than one line\nHere is the second, which al
so has multiple lines..." -et -end-stag -o out.pdf
```

Here is the structure tree:

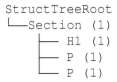

```
StructTreeRoot
└──Section (1)
        ├── H1 (1)
        ├── P (1)
        └── P (1)
```

Some PDF standards require that everything not marked as content (e.g paragraph, figure) etc. is marked as a an artifact. For example, a background image which is the same on every page, or a page border. This tells PDF processors that it is not logical content.

By default, Cpdf with -draw-struct-tree will mark anything not automatically or manually tagged as content as an artifact. Should you wish to disable this, you may use -no-auto-artifacts. Whether or not you use -no-auto-artifacts, you may use -artifact / end-artifact pairs to mark artifacts manually. For example:

```
cpdf -create-pdf AND -draw-struct-tree -draw -no-auto-artifacts
    -artifact -mtrans "50 700" -end-artifact -bt -text "Hello" -et
    -o out.pdf
```

Here we manually tagged the -mtrans as being an artifact. The text section was automatically tagged as a paragraph, and so all content has been tagged or marked as an artifact.

Some tags require a namespace other than the default. You can set the namespace with -namespace, which affects all future tags until reset. Two namespace abbreviations are available: PDF for the default http://iso.org/pdf/ssn namespace and PDF2 for the PDF 2.0 namespace http://iso.org/pdf2/ssn.

Extra information may be added to structure tree nodes with -eltinfo / -end-eltinfo. For example, to set the alternative description for an image, we might write (in JSON format, or prefixing with PDF in PDF format) -eltinfo "Alt=PDF(A large horse)" -image A -end-eltinfo. Multiple items may be set at once, for example Alt, ActualText, Lang etc.

A role map, which maps non-standard structure types to standard ones, may be set with -rolemap. For example -rolemap "/S1/H1/S2/H2" would map the S1 structure type to the standard type H1 and so on.

Chapter 19

Accessible PDFs with PDF/UA

```
cpdf -print-struct-tree in.pdf

cpdf -extract-struct-tree in.pdf -o out.json

cpdf -replace-struct-tree in.json in.pdf -o out.pdf

cpdf -verify "PDF/UA-1(matterhorn)" [-json] in.pdf

cpdf -verify "PDF/UA-1(matterhorn)" -verify-single <test> [-json] in.pdf

cpdf -mark-as ["PDF/UA-1" | "PDF/UA-2"] in.pdf -o out.pdf

cpdf -remove-mark ["PDF/UA-1" | "PDF/UA-2"] in.pdf -o out.pdf

cpdf -create-pdf-ua-<1|2> <title> [-create-pdf-pages <n>]
      [-create-pdf-papersize <paper size>] -o out.pdf
```

PDF/UA (Universal Accessibility) is a PDF subformat whose rules consist of a set of machine-checkable and human-checkable-only requirements to make PDF documents accessible for all users - for example, those using screen readers. Cpdf has some basic facilities for manipulating the extra PDF constructs which are used in (amongst others) PDF/UA, and a basic verifier for many of the machine-checkable requirements.

19.1 Structure trees

In a PDF document, the optional Structure Tree is a parallel construct which describes the logical structure of a document (as opposed to the information for rendering the document on the screen or printing it out, which every PDF of course contains.)

We can print an abbreviated form of the structure tree to standard output:

```
cpdf -print-struct-tree in.pdf
```

This might yield:

```
StructTreeRoot
└── Document
        ├── Sect
        │      ├── P (1)
        │      │      ├── Span (1)
        │      └── Figure (1)
        ├── Sect
        │      ├── H1 (2)
        │      └── TOC
        │              ├── TOCI
        │              │      └── P
        │              │              └── Link (2)
        .      .
        .      .
        .      .
```

The numbers in parentheses are the page numbers for structure elements, where present. We can extract the full structure tree to JSON for inspection or manupulation:

```
cpdf -extract-struct-tree in.pdf -o out.json
```

Here is a typical fragment:

```
[
  [ 0, { "/CPDFJSONformatversion": 1, "/CPDFJSONpageobjnumbers": [ 52 ] } ],
  [
    102,
    {
      "/Type": { "N": "/StructElem" },
      "/S": { "N": "/TD" },
      "/P": 98,
      "/Pg": 52,
      "/K": { "I": 38 },
      "/T": { "U": "row #7, col #3" },
      "/A": {
        "/O": { "N": "/Layout" },
        "/Height": { "F": 18.28 },
        "/Width": { "F": 73.07689999999999 }
      }
    }
  ],
  [
    15,
    {
      "/Type": { "N": "/StructElem" },
      "/S": { "N": "/TD" },
```

```
      "/P": 59,
      "/Pg": 52,
      "/K": { "I": 20 },
      "/T": { "U": "row #3, col #5" },
      "/A": {
        "/O": { "N": "/Layout" },
        "/Height": { "F": 18.28 },
        "/Width": { "F": 73.07689999999999 }
      }
    }
  ],
...
```

This JSON file contains the structure tree objects from the file, using the format described in chapter 15. There is a special entry in object 0 which gives the key to the page object numbers. In this example, there is one page with object number 52.

This JSON file can be edited, for example to change text strings, and reapplied to the same file from which it was extracted:

```
cpdf -replace-struct-tree out.json in.pdf -o out.pdf
```

If extra objects are required, they should be introduced with negative object numbers: Cpdf will renumber them on import so as not to clash with any existing numbers.

To remove a structure tree from a PDF, we can use -remove-dict-entry from Chapter 20, in other words:

```
cpdf -remove-dict-entry /StructTreeRoot in.pdf -o out.pdf
```

19.2   Verifying conformance to PDF/UA

Cpdf contains a new, experimental verifier for PDF/UA via most of the machine-checkable subset of the Matterhorn Protocol, a list of checks based on the PDF/UA-1 specification. For example, we can run:

```
cpdf -verify "PDF/UA-1(matterhorn)" in.pdf
```

We see:

```
06-001 UA1:7.1-8 Document does not contain an XMP metadata stream
07-001 UA1:7.1-9 ViewerPreferences dictionary of the Catalog dictionary does
not contain a DisplayDocTitle entry
11-006 UA1:7.2-3 Natural language for document metadata cannot be determined.
("No top-level /Lang")
28-004 UA1:7.18.1-4 An annotation, other than of subtype Widget, does not
have a Contents entry and does not have an alternative description (in the
```

```
form of an Alt entry in the enclosing structure element).
28-008 UA1:7.18.3-1 A page containing an annotation does not contain a Tabs
entry
28-011 UA1:7.18.5-1 A link annotation is not nested within a <Link> tag.
28-012 UA1:7.18.5-2 A link annotation does not include an alternate
description in its Contents entry.
```

The first column here is the Matterhorn Protocol checkpoint, the second the reference in the PDF/UA-1 standard docunment, the third the textual description from the Matterhorn Protocol, and an optional fourth (in parentheses) any extra information available.

The same information is available in JSON format by adding -json to the command line:

```
[
  {
    "name": "06-001",
    "section": "UA1:7.1-8",
    "error": "Document does not contain an XMP metadata stream",
    "extra": null
  },
  {
    "name": "07-001",
    "section": "UA1:7.1-9",
    "error": "ViewerPreferences dictionary of the Catalog dictionary does not
contain a DisplayDocTitle entry",
    "extra": null
  },
  {
    "name": "11-006",
    "section": "UA1:7.2-3",
    "error": "Natural language for document metadata cannot be determined.",
    "extra": "No top-level /Lang"
  },
  {
    "name": "28-004",
    "section": "UA1:7.18.1-4",
    "error": "An annotation, other than of subtype Widget, does not have a
Contents entry and does not have an alternative description (in the form of
an Alt entry in the enclosing structure element).",
    "extra": null
  },
  {
    "name": "28-008",
    "section": "UA1:7.18.3-1",
    "error": "A page containing an annotation does not contain a Tabs entry",
    "extra": null
  },
  {
    "name": "28-011",
    "section": "UA1:7.18.5-1",
    "error": "A link annotation is not nested within a <Link> tag.",
    "extra": null
```

```
  },
  {
    "name": "28-012",
    "section": "UA1:7.18.5-2",
    "error": "A link annotation does not include an alternate description in
its Contents entry.",
    "extra": null
  }
```

If verifying many files for a single fault, we may choose which test to run by adding `-verify-single <testname>` to the command line. For example:

```
cpdf -verify "PDF/UA-1(matterhorn)" -verify-single "28-012" in.pdf
```

A list of Matterhorn tests and their implementation status forms Appendix C.

19.3 PDF/UA compliance markers

Once we are sure a file complies to PDF/UA, in terms of both machine and human checks, we can mark it as such:

```
cpdf -mark-as "PDF/UA-1" in.pdf -o out.pdf
```

Or, for the more recent PDF/UA-2 standard:

```
cpdf -mark-as "PDF/UA-2" in.pdf -o out.pdf
```

To remove such a marker we can use, for example:

```
cpdf -remove-mark "PDF/UA-1" in.pdf -o out.pdf
```

19.4 Merging and splitting PDF/UA files

The `-process-struct-trees` option should always be used in conjunction with any splitting or merging command to preserve PDF/UA compliance. Details are given in chapter 2.

19.5 Creating new PDF/UA files

To create a new PDF/UA-1 file, with A4 portrait paper, one page, and the title `"My Book"`, we may write:

```
cpdf -create-pdf-ua-1 "My Book" -o out.pdf
```

A title is needed for every PDF/UA document (even a blank one) for it to meet the standard. For PDF/UA-2, use `-create-pdf-ua-2` instead. To make it valid, you must also draw a top-level PDF/UA-2 Document tag as described below.

19.6 Drawing PDF/UA files

Cpdf can add PDF/UA structure data when drawing on new PDF/UA files. For example the following produces a valid PDF/UA-1 file with structure information:

```
cpdf -create-pdf-ua-1 "Hello" AND
     -embed-std14 /path/to/fonts -draw-struct-tree
     -draw -bt -text "Hello, World" -et -o out.pdf
```

Note we had to specify embedded fonts to make this a valid PDF/UA-1 file. To make a valid PDF/UA-2 file we must also add a top-level Document structure tag with the appropriate namespace. Here is the PDF/UA-2 version of our file:

```
cpdf -create-pdf-ua-2 "Hello" AND
     -embed-std14 /path/to/fonts -draw-struct-tree
     -draw -namespace PDF2 -stag Document -namespace PDF
     -bt -text "Hello, World" -et -end-stag -o out.pdf
```

See chapter 18 for more details about adding structure information when drawing.

Chapter 20

Miscellaneous

```
cpdf -draft [-boxes] [-draft-remove-only <n>] in.pdf [<range>] -o out.pdf

cpdf -remove-all-text in.pdf [<range>] -o out.pdf

cpdf -blacktext in.pdf [<range>] -o out.pdf

cpdf -blacklines in.pdf [<range>] -o out.pdf

cpdf -blackfills in.pdf [<range>] -o out.pdf

cpdf -thinlines <minimum thickness> in.pdf [<range>] -o out.pdf

cpdf -clean in.pdf -o out.pdf

cpdf -set-version <version number> in.pdf -o out.pdf

cpdf -copy-id-from source.pdf in.pdf -o out.pdf

cpdf -remove-id in.pdf -o out.pdf

cpdf -list-spot-colors in.pdf

cpdf -print-dict-entry <key> in.pdf

cpdf -remove-dict-entry <key> [-dict-entry-search <term>]
     in.pdf -o out.pdf

cpdf -replace-dict-entry <key> -replace-dict-entry-value <value>
     [-dict-entry-search <term>] in.pdf -o out.pdf

cpdf -remove-clipping [<range>] in.pdf -o out.pdf

cpdf -obj[-json] <object specification> in.pdf

cpdf -replace-obj <object specification>=<object> in.pdf

cpdf -extract-stream[-decompress] <obj num> in.pdf [-o out.dat | -stdout]

cpdf -replace-stream <obj num> -replace-stream-with <filename>
     in.pdf -o out.pdf
```

20.1   Draft Documents

The -draft operation removes bitmap (photographic) images from a file, so that it can be printed with less ink. Optionally, the -boxes option can be added, filling the spaces left blank with a crossed box denoting where the image was. This is not guaranteed to be fully visible in all cases (the bitmap may be have been partially covered by vector objects or clipped in the original). For example:

```
cpdf -draft -boxes in.pdf -o out.pdf
```

To remove a single image only, specify -draft-remove-only, giving the name of the image obtained by a call to -image-resolution as described in Section 13.3 and giving the appropriate page. For example:

```
cpdf -draft -boxes -draft-remove-only "/Im1" in.pdf 7 -o out.pdf
```

To remove text instead of images, use the -remove-all-text operation:

```
cpdf -remove-all-text in.pdf -o out.pdf
```

20.2   Blackening Text, Lines and Fills

Sometimes PDF output from an application (for instance, a web browser) has text in colors which would not print well on a grayscale printer. The -blacktext operation blackens all text on the given pages so it will be readable when printed.

This will not work on text which has been converted to outlines, nor on text which is part of a form.

```
cpdf -blacktext in.pdf -o out.pdf
```

The -blacklines operation blackens all lines on the given pages.

```
cpdf -blacklines in.pdf -o out.pdf
```

The -blackfills operation blackens all fills on the given pages.

```
cpdf -blackfills in.pdf -o out.pdf
```

Contrary to their names, all these operations can use another color, if specified with -color.

20.3 Hairline Removal

Quite often, applications will use very thin lines, or even the value of 0, which in PDF means "The thinnest possible line on the output device". This might be fine for on-screen work, but when printed on a high resolution device, such as by a commercial printer, they may be too faint, or disappear altogether. The `-thinlines` operation prevents this by changing all lines thinner than `<minimal thickness>` to the given thickness. For example:

```
cpdf -thinlines 0.2mm in.pdf [<range>] -o out.pdf
```
Thicken all lines less than 0.2mm to that value.

20.4 Garbage Collection

Sometimes incremental updates to a file by an application, or bad applications can leave data in a PDF file which is no longer used. This function removes that unneeded data.

```
cpdf -clean in.pdf -o out.pdf
```

NB: This operation is deprecated. This work is now done by default upon writing any file.

20.5 Change PDF Version Number

To change the pdf version number, use the `-set-version` operation, giving the part of the version number after the decimal point. For example:

```
cpdf -set-version 4 in.pdf -o out.pdf
```
Change file to PDF 1.4.

This does not alter any of the actual data in the file — just the supposed version number. For PDF versions starting with 2 add ten to the number. For example, for PDF version 2.0, use `-set-version 10`.

20.6 Copy ID

The `-copy-id-from` operation copies the ID from the given file to the input, writing to the output.

```
cpdf -copy-id-from source.pdf in.pdf -o out.pdf
```
Copy the id from `source.pdf` to the contents of `in.pdf`, writing to `out.pdf`.

If there is no ID in the source file, the existing ID is retained. You cannot use `-recrypt` with `-copy-id-from`.

20.7   Remove ID

The `-remove-id` operation removes the ID from a document.

```
cpdf -remove-id in.pdf -o out.pdf
```

Remove the ID from in.pdf, writing to out.pdf.

You cannot use `-recrypt` with `-remove-id`.

20.8   List Spot Colours

This operation lists the name of any "separation" color space in the given PDF file.

```
cpdf -list-spot-colors in.pdf
```

List the spot colors, one per line in in.pdf, writing to stdout.

20.9   PDF Dictionary Entries

This is for editing data within the PDF's internal representation. Use with caution. To print a dictionary entry:

```
cpdf -print-dict-entry /URI in.pdf
```

Print all URLs in annotation hyperlinks in in.pdf.

To remove a dictionary entry:

```
cpdf -remove-dict-entry /One in.pdf -o out.pdf
```

Remove the entry for /One in every dictionary in.pdf, writing to out.pdf.

```
cpdf -remove-dict-entry /One -dict-entry-search "\{I : 1\}"
     in.pdf -o out.pdf
```

Replace the entry for /One in every dictionary in.pdf if the key's value is the given CPDFJSON value, writing to out.pdf. Alternatively, prefix PDF to give the value in PDF format.

To replace a dictionary entry, give the replacement value in JSON or format:

```
cpdf -replace-dict-entry /One -replace-dict-entry-value "PDF2"
    in.pdf -o out.pdf
```

Remove the entry for /One in every dictionary in.pdf, writing to out.pdf.

```
cpdf -replace-dict-entry /One -dict-entry-search "\{I : 1\}"
    -replace-dict-entry-value "\{I : 2\}" in.pdf -o out.pdf
```

Remove the entry for /One in every dictionary in.pdf if the key's value is the given value, writing to out.pdf.

20.10   Removing Clipping

The -remove-clipping operation removes any clipping paths on given pages from the file.

```
cpdf -remove-clipping in.pdf -o out.pdf
```

Remove clipping paths in in.pdf, writing to out.pdf.

20.11   Exploring PDFs

The -obj operation prints an object to standard output, given the object number. Number 0 is the trailer dictionary, so we begin there:

```
$ cpdf -obj 0 in.pdf
"<</Root 1256 0 R/Length 588/ID[('\029\\t>\249\157\182F_\153V\175z[\234\196)
('\029\\t>\249\157\182F_\153V\175z[\234\196)]/Info 1351 0 R/Size 1406>>"

$ cpdf -obj 1256 in.pdf
"<</OpenAction 1238 0 R/PageLabels<</Nums[0<</S/r>>16<</S/D>>]>>/PageMode
/UseOutlines/Names 924 0 R/Outlines 838 0 R/Pages 851 0 R/Type/Catalog>>"

$ cpdf -obj 1238 out.pdf
"<</D[1225 0 R/Fit]/S/GoTo>>"
```

Alternatively, we may follow a chain of dictionary entries from the trailer dictionary:

```
$ ./cpdf -obj /Root/Pages/Count cpdfmanual.pdf
"133"
```

We may also begin at a numbered page instead of at the trailer dictionary:

```
./cpdf -obj P20/Resources/Font/F58/BaseFont cpdfmanual.pdf
"/MCBERL+URWPalladioL-Roma"
```

To output data in JSON format instead of PDF format, use -obj-json in place of -obj.

A stream may be extracted with -extract-stream or -extract-stream-decompress, which decompresses it first where possible:

```
$ cpdf -obj 0 hello.pdf
"<</Size 4/Root 4 0 R/ID[(\232\20625\030\179/\176q:O\202\135\176u\137)
(\232\20625\030\179/\176q:O\202\135\176u\137)]>>"

$ cpdf -obj 4 hello.pdf
"<</Type/Catalog/Pages 1 0 R>>"

$ cpdf -obj 1 hello.pdf
"<</Type/Pages/Kids[3 0 R]/Count 1>>"

$ cpdf -obj 3 hello.pdf
"<</Type/Page/Parent 1 0 R/Resources<</Font<</F0<</Type/Font/Subtype/Type1
/BaseFont/Times-Italic>>>>>>/MediaBox[0 0 595.275590551 841.88976378]
/Rotate 0/Contents[2 0 R]>>"

$ cpdf -extract-stream-decompress 2 hello.pdf -stdout
1 0 0 1 50 770 cm BT/F0 36 Tf(Hello, World!)Tj ET
```

By these mechanisms, ad-hoc exploration of PDF files is possible.

We may also edit dictionary entries with -replace-obj by giving an object specification, and the new value in JSON or PDF format (prefix with "PDF" to denote PDF format):

---

cpdf -replace-obj /Root/MarkInfo/Marked=true in.pdf -o out.pdf

Replace or add dictionary entry in in.pdf, writing to out.pdf.

cpdf -replace-obj '/Root/Info/Title=PDF(New title)' in.pdf -o out.pdf

Replace or add dictionary entry in in.pdf, writing to out.pdf.

Any part of the object specification not already present will be fabricated using direct nested dictionaries. For example, if /MarkInfo does not exist in the root dictionary, this command adds /MarkInfo <</Marked true>> to the root dictionary.

Stream contents may be replaced with -replace-stream:

---

cpdf -replace-stream 4 -replace-stream-with in.dat in.pdf -o out.pdf

Replace stream object 4's contents with the contents of in.dat.

The stream dictionary is unaffected, save for any correction to its length entry.

Appendix A

Dates

A.1   PDF Date Format

Dates in PDF are specified according to the following format:

```
D:YYYYMMDDHHmmSSOHH'mm'
```

where:

- YYYY is the year;

- MM is the month;

- DD is the day (01-31);

- HH is the hour (00-23);

- mm is the minute (00-59);

- SS is the second (00-59);

- O is the relationship of local time to Universal Time (UT), denoted by '+', '-' or 'Z';

- HH is the absolute value of the offset from UT in hours (00-23);

- mm is the absolute value of the offset from UT in minutes (00-59).

A contiguous prefix of the parts above can be used instead, for lower accuracy dates. For example:

```
D:2014 (2014)
D:20140103 (3rd January 2014)
```

```
D:201401031854-08'00'
```
 (3rd January 2014, 6:54PM, US Pacific Standard Time)

A.2   XMP Metadata Date Format

These are the possible data formats for `-set-metadata-date`:

```
YYYY
YYYY-MM
YYYY-MM-DD
YYYY-MM-DDThh:mmTZD
YYYY-MM-DDThh:mm:ssTZD
```

where:

`YYYY`	year
`MM`	month (01 = Jan)
`DD`	day of month (01 to 31)
`hh`	hour (00 to 23)
`mm`	minute (00 to 59)
`ss`	second (00 to 59)
`TZD`	time zone designator (`Z` or `+hh:mm` or `-hh::mm`)

Appendix B

Change logs

B.1 Cpdf Change Log

2.8 (December 2024)

New features:

o New -center-to-fit centres pages on a given paper size
o New -jpeg-to-jpeg-scale and -jpeg-to-jpeg-dpi
o Rasterize PDFs by calling out to GhostScript
o Extract pages as PNG/JPEG by calling out to GhostScript
o Replace stream content with -replace-stream

Extended features:

o Expand page characteristics to cover Art, Trim, Bleed
o Add Piece Info to -composition[-json]
o Add @b<n>@ for trimming bookmark text to given length
o Allow bold, italic, colours for JSON bookmarks
o Show OpenAction in -info
o Show more form information in -info
o Allow JSON / PDF syntax in dict processing and object exploration
o Show %Bookmark text when stamping text
o Change units for -info[-json] and -page-info[-json]
o Optionally add dot leaders to tables of content
o Add -collate-n to extend -collate to multiple pages at once

Fixes:

o Clean up @B implementation for -split-on-bookmarks
o -merge-add-bookmarks now has proper titles for images
o Font operations now include fonts within xobjects
o Image extraction now includes images within xobjects within xobjects
* HTML manual now ranks equally with PDF manual

* = Supported by a grant from NLnet

2.7.2 (October 2024)

New features:

```
* New -args-json for better control files
* New -replace-obj to edit dictionary entries via chain
* Create PDF/UA files from scratch with -create-pdf-ua-[1|2]
* Create structure information for files with -draw
* Draw can now make paragraphs with -para, -paras
* Add structure information to -typeset
* -typeset can make PDF/UA documents
* -jpeg, -png and friends can make PDF/UA documents
* Merge PDF/UA-1 and PDF/UA-2 files, preserving standards compliance
o -stretch scales without preserving aspect ratio
o -redact removes whole pages
```

Extended features:

```
o Rectangles may be specified as x y x' y' rather than x y w h
```

Fixes:

```
o Removed setting of Producer field in AGPL version
* Removed long-deprecated -control
* More compact -print-struct-tree
o -image-resolution-json was listing all images
```

```
* = Supported by a grant from NLnet
```

2.7.1 (July 2024)

New features:

```
o Build PDF files from JPEG2000 (.jp2, .jpf/.jpx) files
* Mark a file as PDF/UA compliant, or remove such marking
* Partial verification to PDF/UA via the Matterhorn protocol
* Extract, edit and reapply document structure tree
* Print structure tree summary
* Split structure tree when splitting PDF to save size
* Combine structure trees when merging or stamping PDFs
* Set the natural language of a file
```

Extended features:

```
o Allow -obj to look up nested PDF information
* Merge structure trees better when merging files
* Report top-level natural language on -info
* Report mark information dictionary contents on -info
```

Backward-incompatible change:

```
* -process-struct-tree replaces -no-process-struct-tree
newly introduced in previous version
```

```
* = Supported by a grant from NLnet
```

2.7 (February 2024)

New features:

o Split files to max size with -split-max
o Spray splits a file to multiple outputs by alternating pages
o List document and page info in JSON format
o List page labels in JSON format
o List fonts in JSON format
o Identify PDF/A, PDF/X, PDF/E, PDF/VT, PDF/UA in -info
o Identify AcroForm in -info
o Extract font files from a document
o List images on a page with -list-images[-json]
o Chop pages up into sections with -chop
o Build PDF files from JBIG2 streams, including globals
o Reprocess images within PDFs to further compress them
o Extract streams to disk
o Explore PDFs by printing objects
o Shift page boxes with -shift-boxes

Extended features:

o -list-images-used[-json] extends -image-resolution
o Use -raw with -extract-images to get PNMs
o -extract-images can extract JBIG2 images and their globals
o More PNGs - greyscale 1, 2, 4, 8, 16bpp and RGB 16bpp
o Report number of annotations in -page-info
o Specify image based only on file extension
o -squeeze updates old compression methods
o Show page size summary in -info
o Add -no-process-struct-trees to prevent merging of structure trees

Fixes:

o Added opam file in-source
o Fixed -set-annotations with page links
o Allow Exif JPEGs as well as JFIF ones in -jpeg and -draw-jpeg
o Only compress a stream if it actually makes it smaller

2.6.1 (September 2023)

o Fixed regression in UTF8 text with -add-text´

2.6 (July 2023)

New features:

o Create new PDF documents or draw on existing ones with -draw
o Embed TrueType fonts with -load-ttf
o Embed the 14 standard fonts if requested
o Add links to parts of text with -add-text as %URL[|]
o Convert JPEGs and PNGs to PDFs with -jpeg and -png
o Export, import, and thereby round-trip annotations via JSON
o Show composition of PDF with -composition[-json]
o Use page labels like <iii> and <A-2> in page specifications

Extended features:

o Allow -utf8 with -split-bookmarks -o @B.pdf to produce UTF8 filenames

o -merge-add-bookmarks now works with unicode filenames
o Better transformation of some annotation types
o -list-annotations[-json] now respects page range
o Merge now merges structure trees (tagged PDF)
o Merge now rewrites clashing name tree entries
o Preserve /GoTo actions in bookmarks when merging
o UTF8 option for JSON output
o -info now shows object stream, /ID data, page mode and layout
o More options for viewer preference control
o More default colours, by using the CSS colour list

Fixes:

o Updated Yojson to remove dependency on Stream, ready for OCaml 5
o -typeset was opening files in text mode, instead of binary
o Fixed behaviour of -squeeze-no-pagedata / -squeeze-no-recompress
o Significant improvements to malformed file reading
o Allow DUP page specifications to use larger numbers
o Reworked functions transforming pages to better preserve patterns

2.5.1 (January 2022)

o Fix a regression where standard fonts could not be chosen

2.5 (January 2022)

New features:

o Can read as well as write PDFs in JSON format with -j
o New operation -typeset typesets a text file as a PDF
o New operation -table-of-contents makes table of contents from bookmarks
o New operations -impose and -impose-xy for document imposition
o New operation -print-font-table gives (charcode, unicode, glyph name) triples
o New -print-dict-entry operation prints values for a given key
o New -replace-dict-entry function to search & replace e.g URLs
o Prepend e.g 2DUP to a page range to make 1,2,3 --> 1,1,2,2,3,3 etc.
o Prepend NOT to a page range to invert it
o Output annotations in JSON form with -list-annotations-json
o Output bookmarks in JSON format with -list-bookmarks-json
o Load bookmarks in JSON format with -add-bookmarks-json
o New option -collate to collate pages when merging
o Text added in existing fonts is now encoding-aware (plus new raw mode)

Extended features:

o Extend -remove-dict-entry to allow search
o Annotation /QuadPoints processed in addition to /Rect when transforming pages
o When adding text or graphics, may choose CYMK or Grey instead of RGB
o The -list-fonts operation now obeys the range
o Can now search for a font by real name with -font
o Basic merging of AcroForms when merging documents
o Add -idir-only-pdfs to restrict -idir to just files ending in .pdf
o Option -debug-force now properly documented as -decrypt-force

Internal changes:

o Switch to Yojson for faster/better JSON input/output
o Environment variable CPDF_REPRODUCIBLE_DATES for testing
o Environment variable CPDF_DEBUG for -debug
o Effectively make stderr unbuffered
o Split cpdf.ml into separate modules

2.4 (June 2021)

o New operation -extract-images
o New operation -output-json et al. to export PDF files in JSON format
o New operations to manipulate Optional Content Groups
o New operation -stamp-as-xobject to add one PDF as an xobject in another
o Optional Content Groups now preserved when merging / stamping pages
o Listing, coalescing and modfiying Optional Content Groups.
o New -labels-progress option to improve page labels interface
o Appearance streams transformed when transforming annotations
o Bookmark destination positions transformed when transforming pages
o No longer depends on Bigarray or Unix modules

2.3 (patchlevel 1, December 2019)

o Fixed bug which prevented -info working on encrypted files
o Allow -shift with -add-text for additional adjustment
o Prepend and postpend directly to page content streams

2.3 (October 2019)

o Directly set and remove Trim, Art, and Bleed boxes
o Dump attachments to file
o Extended bookmark format, preserving all bookmark information
o New -pad-with, -pad-mutiple-before options
o Set or create XMP metadata
o Remove graphics clipping
o Extended support for reading malformed files
o Embed missing fonts by calling out to gs
o Set bookmarks open to a given level
o Create PDF files from scatch
o Remove single images by name
o Add trim marks

2.2 (patchlevel 1)

o Fix for inability to read null objects in streams
o Workaround for Adobe "Error 21" on re-saving encrypted files
o More efficient bookmark operations on files with many pages
o New operation -hard-box to clip contents to a given box

2.2 (March 2017)

o Perform arithmetic on dimensions when specifying size or position
o Add simple rectangles to PDF to blank things out
o Stamping operations now preserve annotations
o Decryption fully on-demand for speed.

o -keep-l keeps existing linearization status
o -remove-dict-entry to remove the contents of a dictionary entry
o -topline in addition to -midline
o -producer and -creator may be used to alter producer and creator
in conjunction with any other operation
o -topline and -midline now apply to stamps
o -list-spot-colours
o -bates-at-range and -bates-pad-to
o -print-page-labels
o -squeeze replaces smpdf
o Preserve more sharing of data when doing merges and page alterations

2.1 (December 2014)

o Encryption now much, much faster
o Faster parsing of delayed object streams on large files
o -decompress now leaves object streams decompressed
o Select pages by landscape-ness or portrait-ness in a page range
o New -open-at-page and -open-at-page-fit option to set the open action
o New -recrypt option to re-encrypt output
o Reads XMP metadata and outputs it on -info
o New -center position for text
o -stamp can now use positions, just like stamping text
o Better handling of permissions for files with user passwords
o Linearization excised
o Can encrypt or recrypt output of -split and -split-bookmarks now
o -args replaces -control with better behaviour
o Can scale a stamp to fit before stamping with -scale-stamp-to-fit

B.2   CamlPDF Change Log

(CamlPDF is the library Cpdf is based upon)

2.8 (December 2024)

o Read and write bookmark colour and flags
o Fixed a bug in Pdfst.renumber_parent_trees
o Only call renumber_parent_trees when processing struct trees

2.7.2 (October 2024)

o Process destination name tree in Pdfpage.pdf_of_pages
o Options to change the whitespace between operators
o Allow writing of comments in streams
o Allow addition of top-level Document in struct tree when merging
o New lookup_chain / replace_chain functions in Pdf
o Revert 2.7 "Remember and reapply inline image decode parameters"

2.7.1 (July 2024)

o Fix sign extension in js_of_ocaml
o Pdfannot expanded to more annotation types
o Extract code to Pdftree module (API subject to change)
o Structure tree optionally trimmed on Pdf.pdf_of_pages
o Sturcture tree optionally trimmed & merged in Pdfmerge

2.7 (February 2024)

o Add opam file in-source
o Cope with more malformed bookmarks
o Remember and reapply inline image decode parameters
o Pdfimage extracts and stores JBIG2Globals
o Option to compress a stream only if it is made smaller
o Encode predictor for PNG Sub (bpc = 8, 3 components)
o Fix for LZWDecode streams which overfill the table
o New endpage_fast
o Remove some very old unused Pdfimage code
o Reconstruct tree in Pdfpage.pdf_of_pages for better bookmarks
o Cope with predictor dictionary not being end of inline image dictionary

2.6 (July 2023)

Merging improvements:
o Keep major PDF version number
o Merge /StructTreeRoot entries (Structure hierarchy / Tagged PDF)
o Disambiguate destination name trees when merging
o Preserve named destinations in bookmarks when merging
o Remove /OpenAction on merge
o Preserve first metadata seen on merge

Other:
o Cope with files with no /MediaBox at all
o Write IDs as Hexadecimal strings
o Replace Stream/Genlex and other deprecations for OCaml 5
o Allows malformed numbers --1, --2.5 etc.
o Support for alternative stubs for js_of_ocaml
o Push mk_id down to pdf_to_output so it works when writing to
  non-file destinations
o Fix Pdf.getnum and Pdf.parse_rectangle to cope with indirects
o Ignore data check errors in flate decoding
o Now reads many more files from Stressful PDF Corpus
o Revert 'build byte code top level camlpdf.top by default'
o Pdfpage.add_prefix now detects and fixes non-ISO PDFs
o Loosen EI check on inline image lexing
o Compress inline images upon writing if uncompressed
o Retired old unused modules to old/
o Cope with /Crypt identity filters
o Ability to redirect error output
o Harden ASCII85Decode against whitespace

2.5 (January 2022)

o Build byte code top level camlpdf.top by default
o Replace deprecated C interface functions for OCaml 5.0
o Document most undocumented functions
o Pdfpage.change_pages now preserves object streams
o Width calculation in Pdfstandard14 now more efficient
o Charcode and text extractors have font not fontdict counterparts
o Pdftext.charcode_extractor_of_font copes with more encodings
o Add Pdftext.simplify_utf16be
o Merge now merges AcroForms
o Fix Pdfio.setinit and friends to deal with 0-length data
o Harden Pdfmarks against erroneous empty /Title in doc outline

o AFM and glyphlists loaded from compressed sources
o Environment variable CAMLPDF_REPRODUCIBLE_IDS for testing
o Effectively make stderr unbuffered for all output
o A dictionary entry with null for its value now does not exist
o A missing mediabox now not fatal - we use the most-recently-seen

2.4 (June 2021)

o Prefixed all C stubs to avoid clashes with zlib / cryptokit
o Fix for zero-sized Pdfio.input_outputs
o Bad interaction between deferred decryption and object streams fixed
o Optional content groups merged when merging
o Pdfpage.change_pages can now alter bookmark destinations for transformed pages
o Preserves zero bytes in malformed names
o Merged files get fresh /ID
o Pdfpagelabels.write now removes labels when given an empty list

2.3 (patchlevel 2, 2020)

o Bad interaction between deferred decryption and object streams worked around

2.3 (patchlevel 1, December 2019)

o Updated Makefile to build on bytecode-only architectures
(thanks Ralf Treinen)

2.3 (October 2019)

o Malformed file reading for files with content before the header now works
o Switches to disable malformed file reading or always read as if malformed
o Fix to preserve integers > 2^30 or < -2^30 on 32 bit systems
o Allow [/DCT] as well as /DCT in inline image filter specifications
o Improvements to text width calculation (thanks Alain Frisch)

2.2 (patchlevel 1, September 2017)

o Code for adding annotations (thanks @waclena)
o Indirect encryption dictionaries
o Workaround for Adobe "Error 21" on re-saving encrypted files
o Fix reading of null objects in streams

2.2 (2017)

o Keeps was_linearized flag with every loaded PDF

2.1 (November 2014)

o Excised linearization. We recommend qpdflib / qpdf for this task now.
o Encryption now performed by fast C routines, replacing the OCaml ones
o Faster parsing of delayed object streams on large files
o New implementation of Pdf.page_reference_numbers. More robust
o Faster parsing by using better primitive operations for I/O
o Tighter spacing of output in Pdfwrite leading to smaller files
o Fixed pdf_of_pages not to produce duplicate page objects when multiple parts
of the output pdf come from the same input pdf
o Pdfpagelabels bug fixes, especially to alphabetic labels
o Read StemV etc. values from the AFM header directly
o Object streams may be written uncompressed for manual inspection

o Recrypting overhauled. Now a first class citizen.

1.7 (30th August 2013)

o Support for writing with object streams
o AES256ISO encryption support
o More compact writing of files
o Support for reading many malformed files
o Now under a standard LGPL license
o Has no dependencies
o First import into git for use with GitHub for open development
o Support for ocamlfind

Appendix C

Matterhorn Protocol

Implementation status:

```
Fully implemented:
  01-007
  02-001 02-003 02-004
  06-001 06-002 06-003
  07-001 07-002
  09-004 09-005 09-006 09-007 09-008
  11-006
  13-004
  14-002 14-003 14-006 14-007
  15-003
  17-002
  19-003 19-004
  20-001 20-002 20-003
  21-001
  25-001
  26-001 26-002
  28-002 28-004 28-006 28-007 28-008 28-009 28-010 28-011 28-012 28-014
          28-015 28-016 28-017
  30-001
  31-001 31-002 31-003 31-004 31-005 31-006 31-017 31-019 31-020 31-021
          31-022 31-023 31-024 31-025 31-026 31-028 31-029

Partially implemented:
  31-009 31-027

Unimplemented:
  01-003 01-004 01-005
  10-001
  11-001 11-002 11-003 11-004 11-005
  17-003
  28-005 28-018
  30-002
  31-007 31-008 31-011 31-012 31-013 31-014 31-015 31-016 31-018 31-030
```